ALABAMA BOUND

"Justice Without Politics"

FROM A BILLBOARD SLOGAN
DURING THE 1974 CAMPAIGN FOR
CIRCUIT JUDGE, MOBILE COUNTY

ALABAMA BOUND

FORTY-FIVE YEARS INSIDE A PRISON SYSTEM

Ray A. March

THE UNIVERSITY OF ALABAMA PRESS
UNIVERSITY, ALABAMA

PHOTO CREDITS
The photographs in the text of this volume were taken by
Ray A. March and Christina Hudson.
The photographs following the index were taken by
Brad Fisher.

Library of Congress Cataloging in Publication Data

Main entry under title:

Alabama bound.

   1. Prisons—Alabama. 2. Punishment—Alabama.
3. Corrections—Alabama. 4. Prisons—Alabama—
Officials and employees—Interviews. I. March,
Ray A., 1934–
HV9475.A2A5   365'.9761   77-3352
ISBN 0-8173-4406-3

CONTENTS

ACKNOWLEDGMENTS

It took Oscar Dees, his son Fred Dees, and his grandson Fred Dees, Jr., to do this book. It's theirs, for without their understanding and cooperation it obviously could not have been written. I would also like to acknowledge the Dees women, who are also special people, particularly Jennie Dees, who always offered just the right "observations."

There were many helpers who prodded and poked me to complete this work, notably: Gordon Bryars and John Leake, who gave me the idea and the entrée; my group at the UCLA sensitivity session at Ojai in the summer of 1975, especially Iral, Bill L., and Marty, who all said I should "get on with it"; Stan and Nancy Cloud, who gave me a good push on the first draft; Sue Cleaver, another nomad who has a special quality and silent way of giving encouragement, and who, in addition, typed most of the correspondence; Verva Densmore, who typed the first inquiries; Carol Cox, who found extra time to help; G. L. and Bing Ray, for providing cabin space during the final editing and for advice on roughage; Steve Gann, who kept calling about my health; attorney David R. Coley III, of Mobile, for his generous legal assistance; and to Alabama State Representative Brooks Hines, the Civil Liberties Union of Alabama, the Southern Poverty Law Center, and the Southern Prison Ministry for research efforts and information.

Most importantly, though, my gratitude goes to Kris Hudson, who with great patience and editing skill kept it all in perspective for me. Thank you.

PREFACE

On January 13, 1976, United States District Court Judge Frank M. Johnson, Jr., declared the entire Alabama prison system to be unconstitutional.

His order, encompassing a broad area, gave Governor George Wallace, the Alabama legislature, state officials, and prison authorities four months to two years in which to reform the system so as to meet a number of specific minimum constitutional standards.

The court's decision came as a result of a class-action suit filed on behalf of Alabama prison inmates. The judge found that inmates were indeed being deprived of their rights under the Eighth and Fourteenth amendments, which prohibit, respectively, the imposition of cruel and unusual punishment and denial of due process of the law and the equal protection of the laws.

In his memorandum opinion, covering eleven major areas of treatment of prisoners, Judge Johnson stated unequivocally: "The living conditions in Alabama prisons constitute cruel and unusual punishment." While observing emphatically that "prisoners are not to be coddled, and prisons are not to be operated as hotels or country clubs," the judge stated that "this does not mean that responsible state officials, including the Alabama legislature, can be allowed to operate prison facilities that are barbaric and inhumane."

Judge Johnson placed all the defendant state officials on notice: "Failure to comply with the minimum standards set forth in the order of this court," his order stated, "will necessitate the closing of those several prison facilities . . . found to be unfit for human confinement."

The minimum standards set forth dealt specifically with overcrowding; segregation and isolation; classification of inmates; mental health care; protection from violence; living conditions; food service; correspondence and visitation, educational, vocational, work and recreational opportunities; and physical facilities and staff. With respect to the last of these, the judge ordered the establishment of an affirmative-action hiring program.

It should be emphasized at the outset that the idea for this book
and the interviews on which it is based antedated Judge Johnson's
court order by some two years. The book is in no way intended
to be a response to, or a commentary on, that court order or the
findings of fact on which it was based.

The book is, in fact, simply the recollections and reflections
of three men—Oscar Dees, his son, Fred H. Dees, Sr., and his
son (and Oscar Dees' grandson), Fred H. Dees, Jr.—who have,
collectively, worked more than forty-five years in various capac-
ities in the Alabama corrections system—as warden, as road-
camp superintendent, as probation/parole officer, among others.

The experiences and philosophies they recount begin in 1931,
when use of the "strap" was a common mode of punishment,
and range forward in time to the civil-rights movements of the
1960s, present-day prison conditions, and rehabilitation and
probation techniques as they exist in Alabama.

These accounts are based on interviews with members of the
Dees family from 1974 through early 1976. The interviews were
very informal, often taking place during meals, while riding in
a pickup truck, or while fishing the back reaches of the Tensaw
River or the wilderness of the bayou country northeast of Mobile,
Alabama.

The sessions were unstructured. There was no sequence of
questions intentionally designed to develop a chronological
order. Because of this informality, a subject frequently was re-
turned to long after it was originally discussed and these subse-
quent interviews usually clarified places, names, and dates.

The comments of all the participants were taped, and occasionally I made notes, taped or written, to remind myself to return
to a subject and explore it further. As transcribed, the tapes
amounted to approximately five hundred pages of unedited man-
uscript; the transcription was then indexed and cross-referenced,
first by individual then by subject.

The next step was to edit the transcript by ordering subject
matter chronologically. This procedure enabled me to pursue
certain areas in more depth after I had determined their importance in the overall development of the oral history.

I have retained many of the colloquialisms used, but have not attempted to record the participants' Alabama dialect; any such attempt would serve only to distract the reader. Only minor revisions were made in sentence structure and the like, here and there, taking into account the needs of readers (as distinct from listeners) in readily grasping what was being said.

With the exception of towns, prisons, places, and certain prominent people, all names have been changed not only to protect the privacy of those still living, but also to save unknowing families from possible embarrassment. While this work was being compiled Atmore prison was renamed by the Alabama Board of Corrections in honor of the late Warden Green Kendrick Fountain because the Atmore city council protested that the city was receiving unfavorable publicity.

Vallejo, California   RAY A. MARCH

To my daughters,

Michelle and Melissa,

known among Tensaw River folk as

"Big M" and "Little M"

1 OSCAR DEES

A veteran of thirty-eight years in the Alabama

prison system, a retired warden, talks

about prison life—about punishment, the electric

chair, and rehabilitation.

OSCAR DEES, NOW RETIRED, HOLDING AN ENLARGED PHOTOGRAPH
OF THE OLD KILBY PRISON WHERE HE WAS ONCE DEPUTY WARDEN.

The little cabin, with its

screened front sleeping porch, rests partly on cement blocks, partly on stilts, and leans out over the bluff. Below, small fibreglass fishing boats rock gently at their berths under wooden sunshades. Occasionally, a fisherman idles out to the main waterways and secluded bays for his catch of bass, catfish, bream, or goggle-eye.

This is southern Alabama bayou country. Fed by the Alabama, Tombigbee, Mobile, and Tensaw rivers, the bayou stretches for hundreds of miles in all directions, connected by canals, bays, and creeks. Until you're on the water you don't know how much there is because much of it is hidden. Spanish moss shrouds the passages, and great tall trees cling by tangled roots to what solid substance they can find. When you move quietly, barely skimming the water, you can see black-shelled turtles sunning, an occasional water moccasin matching itself to a limb, and, if you're quick, an alligator submerging.

This country and its people dominate how you think, what you do, and who you are. It's a good place to rest, fish, and talk. There is a slow pace here, and interruptions come only when a squawking big-domed bluejay makes its entrance or when it's time to eat or go fishing again. It was here, in this water-born country, next to the cabin, that Oscar Dees began to tell his story.

He sat at a metal picnic table under oak trees hung with the ever-present moss. Dees, a hulking six-foot four and two-hundred-eighty pounds, straddled the bench while Fred and Jennie, his son and daughter-in-law, sat off to the right in outdoor metal rockers. Cracking and pinching hot roasted peanuts from a tray on the table, Dees, in a soft and polite voice, began to describe his thirty-eight years in the Alabama prison system. He made a point in the beginning to apologize for "talking like a nigger" because of his years in the prisons, but he said it with a laugh as if he didn't really mean to apologize at all. This first day, and always, he spoke with great chivalry, with care in his choice of words and expressions. Only in later privacy did it become apparent that he would not discuss conjugal visits or the electric chair in front of women. Those discussions and others took place while driving across acres of the Atmore Prison Farm or at his home.

No matter where Oscar Dees was, there was always a rambling of talk as he reminisced and collected thoughts and time, often with the help of

Fred and Jennie; he felt no need for organization or to relate one matter to another.

"They done away with the strap and decided they would use some other method of discipline. So they got to burning up the cotton mill; every night [at Kilby] they'd set the cotton mill afire. I was at Ketona at that time running a road camp, and they sent after me and the governor called me out there and says, 'We got to stop this mill being burned up, it's costing us too much money, we just can't afford to have it.' They hadn't mentioned anything about any other kind of discipline, so I went home and got me some hose pipe and carried it down there in solitary confinement to where I could use it. I went to the dining room that evening—the shift that went to work at three o'clock was doing the burning up of the mill—so, I got up on the stage in the dining room and told them that I didn't want them burning up the mill to cost them anything: I was going to furnish the matches. All I wanted them to do was furnish the heads and whatever it took to go with it, that they wasn't going to burn that cotton mill up no more. So I says, 'Now I'm going to punish every prisoner if he comes out of that mill until I get the right one tonight, if you set it afire.' So, they went out and that mill hasn't been burned up no more since then."

Discipline, enforced by punishment or the threat of it, was Oscar Dees' code. You didn't have to agree with him, but he convinced you that he believed in what he said. To his prisoners, Dees must have personified the fear of God. Prisoners and guards alike called him "Big O," "Big D," and "Big Diesel."

He once said: "It all boils down to this point: Where you got discipline you got control; that goes for homes, churches, towns, or whatever you want it. If you hadn't got any discipline, you hadn't got anything."

He suggested that Atmore prison officials today should use the Bible as a guide: ". . . use the rod, don't spare the rod," Dees advised.

"It don't say a thing about the strap," Jennie answered.

"It don't say nothing about no strap, but it says something about that rod," Dees replied, "and that rod can be used as a strap or an oak limb or whatever you want to call it!" In Dees' view, punishment is one way of "getting a man's attention."

"Did you get Fred's attention when he was young," Jennie asked.

"Many!" Fred offered.

"One time!" corrected Dees.

"Many times!" Fred insisted, jokingly, and without elaboration.

Oscar Dees retired in 1969 to a tidy two-bedroom home he had built on a three-acre parcel just ten miles from the town of Atmore. He lives there with his wife, who works at a downtown drugstore. They affectionately call each other "George."

The land around their house is flat with an occasional roll. During the spring and humid summer it's kept a lush green by cooling showers. An inviting land, it's the kind on which even an amateur can be confident that something will grow from seed. Some years Dees, a farmer before he was a warden, plants part of his land in corn, and he usually raises two or three calves to be sold at local auction. But it's more a hobby than a means of income because he says there isn't much money in it.

It was here, in the comfort of his land, seen from the enclosed patio of his home, that he spoke his mind the most freely, not limiting his views to the Alabama prison system, but entwining them with opinions on politics, the press, the state of the nation, and pride in his Atmore friends. When he spoke of his past, he did so in consistently even tones, but when he talked of politics or the press he was vehement.

"I'm going to tell you right now," Oscar Dees said, "the trouble with our country today, with the penitentiary system and most everything else, is our press. Our press is just as one-sided as it can be. I heard in there on the television this morning that Howard Hughes, [the one] they're raising sand about—this was a Republican talking—says they're raising sand about Howard Hughes giving Nixon a hundred thousand dollars. He give Humphrey fifty thousand dollars. He says, 'Why don't the press get on Humphrey?' Says, 'He's a Democrat, they're on Republicans, they're on Nixon, and they ain't said nothing about Humphrey,' and he says, 'Howard Hughes give Humphrey fifty thousand dollars, and he give Nixon a hundred thousand dollars.' So, it's the press is what blows things all out of proportion, and what stirs the people up."

"And on the other hand," Fred Dees countered, "we're the cause of that because we don't let the press know really what's going on."

"No, 'cause we had an open book when we was using the strap," Oscar Dees argued. "They could walk in and look at the records and see who got punished."

"But you wouldn't let 'em inside the penitentiary 'cause the doghouse was used."

"No, ah, I did it. I let the judge and the solicitor both out of Mobile go, but it was . . ."

"But, you wouldn't let the press go."

"No, I wouldn't let the press go."

"So, he had to imagine what was going on."

"Well, he wouldn't tell the truth if he did *know what was going on!"*
And the elder laughed loud and long, and nothing more was said about it.

*On rides into town Oscar Dees greeted friends with warm enthusiasm
and they responded to his jovial mood.*

"Hello, Scotty! Let's go fishing, boy!"

"You better get over there," Scotty yelled back.

"Yeah?"

"Yeah, they're eating it up!"

*He feels very much a part of this small agricultural community, and
as he drives around town he talks of his civic work, of being a member of
a local water-district board, of being a Shriner and a church-attending
Baptist. His heritage is in this country. He was born here and, as a boy,
he farmed here; he began his prison career here; and he came back to
retire here.*

*"I'll tell you, I have really got the friends around Atmore. This is a
friendly little ol' town. I got a first cousin that runs a cucumber shed, that
shed right up yonder. They farm a world of cucumbers here, make them
into pickles. They put them in the brine and all, and then they take them
to Montgomery, I think it is. Now, that's where our sister lives, right
there." And he went on, pointing out family, friends, country places.*

Oscar Dees

Robinsonville. Named after my granddaddy. Robinsonville. Just
east of Atmore. Back yonder where the graveyard was, that's Robinsonville. Well now, my granddaddy was named Robinson.
When he moved to that country, right there, was where my mother
and them was raised. When he moved there, there was three
houses between that and Atmore—just five miles, just three
houses. He was a lumberman, run a sawmill and farmed some
too. Mostly a sawmill, and he bought that land, raised some tim-
ber on it, bought it for three dollars an acre. He came in about

1890, somewhere along there, about 1890. That church was built in 1905, and I was born in 1906. My mother's folks I reckons about the oldest families there was in this country.

We didn't have no grass when I was a boy. We hoed it up. We hoed all the grass up. It [the yard] was perfectly clean and just as white. And my grandmother—I never did see this but in one kitchen—my grandmother went on crutches, my grandmother Dees, and she had a pink pipe she smoked, cob pipe with a cane stem in it about that long, and she sat there and smoked. Well, they had a nigger woman that was her maid, and she'd sweep the kitchen like when we got through eating and all, and she swept the kitchen out, and she'd make sand just as white as that shirt you got and sprinkle it all over that kitchen—that sand all over that kitchen. And it was just as white; she swept it off every day after dark, put clean sand on it, and that kitchen was just as white as that thing over yonder. And that's the only time I ever seen it done.

Now, I'll tell you something else. You never seen a boy like I am myself. I carried yellow jackets to the school; I turned them loose, and they got out a loose and the teacher wore long plaited hair and it went down below her waist and them yellow jackets got in them plaits, and me and another ol' boy, well, we just shut the school. That's all there was to it. We just shut the school down and they whupped us, and then she whupped us again. She was staying at the boarding house and she went home and told Momma, and Momma beat the fire out of me again, and here come the board of trustees over there to the house and told Momma that if I didn't change my way of doing they was going to send me to a reform school. But when they cocked that jailhouse door on me I changed my mind! But, that's the way things get started, just thataway. If they probably hadn't whupped me when I turned them yellow jackets loose in that school, if I had got by with that, I would have done something else.

My daddy was dead, and Momma, she was strict; oh good gracious alive, she could whup you worse than Papa could. She'd

draw a ring in the yard with her toe and tell you, "Stand in that
ring." She didn't catch you by the hand. And she'd take one of
these ol' brushbrooms like the nigger woman used. They went
down in the woods and cut some gallberries down and tied a
bunch of them together, about that big around, and swept the
yards with it, see, and she'd just pick up that brushbroom and
take both hands and just whup the fire out of you.

My daddy died when I was ten. He died during the First World
War. No, he wasn't in the war. He was 36 years old and he had
four kids, see.

When they hired me to go to work for the state (that was in
1931), I was plowing a mule out to the end of the row and turned-
up side of the fence. The warden—he was sitting there in a old
car, a old Ford car, asked me did I want to come up there go to
work for the state. 'Course, I knew the warden personally, he
used to be sheriff here. I drove right up to the fence. He called
me Big One, says, "Big One, you want a job with the state?" I says,
"Mr. Fountain, I don't know nothing 'bout no prisons. I don't
know whether I want a job up there or not. I don't know whether
Momma would want me to go up in there now." He says, "Well,
you an orphan boy, you can make more up there supporting
your momma and sisters than you can here farming. You go talk
to your momma and tell her that you can make an easier living
up there than you trying to make on this farm. You tell her I'll
take care of you."
I wasn't but twenty-three years old. Daddy left us twenty-two
acres of land. That's what we worked and made a living on. There
was two boys; I was the oldest—I'm the oldest one in the whole
bunch. There was five of us.
The warden says, "I know you wouldn't do nothing until you
talked it over with your mother, you talk it over with her and
tell her that I said I would look out for you and give you a job
Monday morning if you want to come up there. You tell her I'll
take care of you 'cause I'd sure love to have you." I went home
and talked to Momma about it, and Momma told me, says, "You
can go up there and try it."

The prison yard of the G. K. Fountain Correctional Center, formerly Atmore Prison Farm.

I was married then. I was married then, and I believe I lived with Momma and, let's see, Fred was born after I went to work. Well, they was all born after I went to work for the state. Now, Elaine, she's the oldest. She was a baby when I went to work for the state. That was on Thursday, and I went up there on Monday morning and went to work, and I worked there thirty-eight years.

I started at Atmore, the old Atmore. That's the only prison they had there then.*
After I left the farm my brother worked it. He worked the farm, and I worked over at the prison. And we got along better after I went to work for the state 'cause naturally it was hard going trying to make a living then; that was during the Depression, see. So, it was rough. And during the First World War, oh, I've seen weeks go by that I didn't see a biscuit. We ate corn bread,

---

*The central structure was built in 1929.

'course; Momma could make corn bread as good as cake. Really, by rights, right now, a good piece of muffin bread and some butter and syrup—I'd rather have it than have biscuits. Now, right now. For breakfast, anytime.

The first job I had was carrying a squad out there. They give me six shells, six buckshot shells and a double-barreled shotgun and a trusty to tote some water and wait on me. And I wasn't supposed to let him come up to me, and the deputy warden says, "Don't let them get no closer than so and so to you" (he was pointing to some object or another). When I went to work for them, they'd put the prisoners in the field. In other words, we checked out between daylight and sunup. They sent our food to us in containers out in the field. We stopped an hour and eat dinner right where we was working; then we went right back to work. Then we checked in between sundown and dark. And the prisoners were so tired, whenever night come, we didn't have any trouble with this homosexual and all that sort of stuff 'cause they was too tired. In other words, we had the "okay." We okayed twice the day, every night and every morning. That was the count, head count.

They would be so tired 'til they'd be—we'd call them out and line them up, and we had a platform that was at the foot of the bed for them to sit on to keep them from messing the bed up, and they'd be sitting on that platform and they'd be so tired that they'd lay back on the floor. We could count them by them laying there.

But, to show you that work means more than just one thing, work will take care of a whole lot of your discipline. If you got a tired man he's not going to give you near as much trouble if you got a man that's sitting around and not tired, and storing up some kind of meanness to get into.

I really needed the job 'cause that was during the Depression, like I said, and they started me off at seventy-two dollars a month, and I worked seven days a week from daylight 'til dark; then I drove ten miles back to the tower. I done that for a year 'fore I moved up there, then I moved up there.

I worked at the prison up there twelve years, then I was gone

nine years, no, I was gone nearly nineteen years 'cause I stayed
at Ketona where I was warden nine years and I stayed at Kilby
nine years. I was deputy warden at Kilby. Then I come back to
Atmore and I finished up at Atmore. Thirty-eight years. That
included the time I was a jail inspector. 'Course there was another
year I was suspended, but I'll get to that.

I've had a whole lot of experience. They're going through the
same thing over at the prison now that I went through. With this
experience I was carrying a plow squad at this time and we had
mules. Plow squad. That's a cultivating squad that cultivated
the farm. We had mules at that time. So, I had went into the shop
and we had to change the different plow on the stock to plow
something else. So, while the prisoners was getting ready to plow
whatever it was I was going to plow, farm whatever it was I was
going to farm, the deputy warden comes by and says, "Come on,
let's go over to Camp Nine." They had hired a man from Georgia
that was going to make them rich on tomatoes. He was a fella
big as me, and we went over there. We didn't have but one tractor;
a great big red nigger was driving it. We drove up over there
and the nigger was standing there by the tractor. That deputy
warden asked him, says, "Red, where's the tomato man?" He says,
"He's gone to camp, Captain." Deputy warden says, "What you
think about that tomato man?" He says, "Well, Captain a man
don't know, he just don't know—that's what I think about him."

Well, you know, that's in every day life—a man don't know,
he just don't know. That's what's wrong today. They got folks on
the job that just don't know. Good folks is one thing and prison
people is another thing. And I fully believe the Lord made us all,
and He made us all for different type work. If we was all made
for the same kind of work, we'd all be cut out for the same kind
of work.

I think there's prison men, there's law enforcement men, there's
preachers, there's doctors, there's judges, there's bankers, whatever you have. And if you're cut out to fill one of them positions
you can do it; if you're not—it's just like a wheel that got a gog
broke out of it. I think they can hire good sheriffs, good police-
mans, good majors, good captains that's made a marvelous record

in their work, but put them in a prison system—they just as lost as a man that's in an airplane that never has run an airplane. There's all the difference in the work; there's no comparison in the work of a law enforcement man and a prison man.

I had a brother-in-law that went to work up there at Atmore, and him and another fella, they had a ol' bunch of men supposed to be cripples, just ol' crippled prisoners, and they went over there to fix a bridge across a little ol' ditch and one of them had a gun and the other didn't have a gun, so an ol' crippled boy that they thought there wasn't a bit of harm in the world in, took that gun away from that other one and then took a truck—took both the guards and all of them, and carried them into Florida, the whole outfit!

'Course, that goes back to guards, that goes back to what I said while ago, if a man is cut out to be a guard it don't take very much to show him and tell him how to guard prisoners. If he's not cut out to handle labor and not cut out to handle prisoners, then all the teaching and all the money you want to spend on him is not going to make a prison man out of him. Just give me a man with good common sense and a man that you can talk to, and that's the man that'll make you the best prison man.

One of the first things they warned me about was what they call "putting the hat on a man." That means a con man. They got some professional con men in the penitentiary. They can make it so plain, and tell you so plain, and make you believe that he hasn't done one thing, that he went to Sunday school every Sunday and was raised in the church, and the only time that he was at home was just to eat. The rest of the time he was in the church; in fact, they arrested him in church, and he ain't guilty of a thing in the world, and they had just railroaded him in there. That's what you call putting the hat on a man—and never let a man tell you that they can't put the hat on him 'cause they'll put the hat on him.

Every convict, when he first gets in the penitentiary, he gets religion. He gets the Bible, and he'll tote that Bible. Literally.

He'll tote it, he'll read it until the day that you call him up there to discharge and tell him to get his personal stuff. Then he'll leave the Bible there. If you check his personal stuff and you ask him, you say, "Joe," or "John," or whatever his name was, "where's your Bible? You've been so faithful since you've been in the penitentiary with the Bible, why are you leaving it?" He leaves it there, he don't carry it with him. And when he comes back he'll pick that same Bible up, too. If they've changed warden or changed any of the officials, he'll pick that same Bible up, and he'll use that same Bible, and he'll put the hat on somebody else.

I was told about that hat deal, so if they didn't make him a trusty, then, far as I was concerned, he was under the gun.

Now, I've had them come to me with all this sort of stuff. Go out to work and he'd say, "Hey there, Captain, I have spells, I have eplictics and I starts a running when I have an eplictic. Would you shoot me if I had an eplictic and started running?" I says, "You'd better run 'round and 'round me if you don't want me to shoot you. If you start off running I'm going to shoot you." So, I broke up that eplictic stuff. 'Course, I've had them have some kind of fits, but they'd just fall over and have them, and I'd get him in the shade and pour some water on him and take care of him.

I had one up there at Ketona that they sent everywhere else, and he could throw a fit and he could fool the doctors—he fooled the doctors for a long time. They really thought he had a fit. So, they sent him to me and first day I sent him out on a job he fell off—he didn't fall off the truck—the truck was stopped and he got down off the truck—he didn't hurt himself—got down off the truck, had him a fit, slobbered at the mouth, and all that sort of stuff. Well, they brought him in and told me they had a prisoner that had a fit.

Well, I had a doctor look at him. The doctor said he couldn't find nothing wrong with him. So, I sent him out the next day and he had another one. I called Montgomery and told them I had a prisoner up there that had fits. I couldn't remember when that was. They told me to bring him to Montgomery. I carried him a hundred miles to Montgomery and they had it made up,

the warden did at Montgomery, did he'd have him to have a fit
whenever he come in the office. They'd done found it out down
there that he was faking, but I didn't know it. So, the warden
told him, made a motion for him to have that fit, and he fell over,
begin to puke and raise sand and all that sort of stuff, and I told
them just wrap him up, I'll take him right now! Right now. I told
him when we left for Ketona, I says, "Now you've had your last
fit 'less I ask you to have one, 'cause if you have one I'm going to
have one, and it ain't going to do for both of us to have a fit at the
same time." And I didn't have no more trouble with him all these
days!

I guarded plow squads and later on a field squad, and that was
when the warden at Atmore asked me to train the dogs. They
had a dog warden from Monroe County, didn't know much about
dogs. Well, I didn't know much about dogs, either, only just fox
dogs and rabbit dogs and things like that. And this fella was a
sheriff and he come down and got the dog job and he was bad to
run after women, and he got to running after these Indian girls
over here. And the warden wanted him one evening, so he went
to looking for him and couldn't find him. So they took him off of
that job, and I was carrying a field squad and he called me in there
—I wasn't even, had never thought about running no dogs—he
called me in there and says, "Dees, I want you to take these dogs
and run them. You know this country and everybody knows you,
I want you to take them and run them."

Well, I took the dogs, and they were sure set in their ways. The
other fella had treed a prisoner in the same place, and training
them he had crossed the creek at the same place; he had run to the
same tree and treed over there at the Indian Reservation. So when
the dogs would get pretty close to that tree they'd just leave the
track and go to the tree. Same way where he crossed the creek—
they'd just go pretty close to where he'd crossed the creek with
them so much, they'd just leave the track and go across the creek.
Well, I had to break them of that.

So, I went to work with them. I told the warden I'd take the
job if he wanted me to, I'd take it. I went to working and training
them, and I got my own ideas about how to train them to where

I could track a man. If the dogs couldn't track him, I could track him; like he come across a oak grove, I could track him by the leaves or something he put on or rubbed his feet or something like that. I could keep the dogs on the right track. I done that to where I could depend on the dogs running without me. I worked with them a year 'fore I got them running where I could really depend on them.

I had a bloodhound and redbone and mixed, 'bout half and half. A bloodhound is too slow and he don't bark much. A red-bone barks good and he trees good and he'll bite you, too. And that ol' bloodhound won't bite you much. Some of them dogs will bite, some of them will bite *you*. I had some that would really bite you, then I had some that was good tree dogs; then I had some dogs that wouldn't bite you, wouldn't bark at a man up a tree either. I bred and raised all my own dogs. I used a thorough-bred male bloodhound with a redbone female. I usually had 'bout thirty-five, and I generally had enough dogs trained that if a bunch of men was to run and some more would run thinking maybe that I didn't have enough to run them, I always had enough dogs that I could be running three, four bunches of men at the same time.

You trained your puppies by dropping a switch. When you crossed a road like that there you dropped that switch across that road where I could track it myself. If the dogs got off on somebody else's track—it's different from running a man and running a fox or a rabbit or something like that—but you got to run the right man, see. There'll be some more men tracks down there, but the dog's got to stay on the right one. I'd have a trusty drop something along his track where I could track it and if the dog got off on another man's track, I'd make him come back and get on that one, and that would teach him not to get off on another man's track—stay on that same track. But you've got to have a reasonable place for a dog to get familiar with the scent of that track 'fore he can take it through other tracks, 'cause some folks think that he can just smell of a handkerchief or something like that—ain't no such dog as that. That's movie stuff!

If I had a prisoner was run away and the dog boy crossed, if he thought maybe that I had got lost from him (that dog boy is

another prisoner running along behind the dogs, staying up
with them on his foot), he'd drop a branch in the road pointing
the way that he was going if I was to get behind and come along
and run into it, see. I'd know he'd crossed that road and gone on
in that direction. And then if I was running a sham race, and if
the prisoners didn't run enough to keep the dogs trained, I run
them three, four times a week. I'd let the prisoners that was training the dogs, putting out a sham race, drop a branch in the road
so when I crossed the road I'd know that he was on the right
track. So in other words, you had to check on your dogs just like
you was checking on anything else to see if you was right!

I used trusties. The trusties would put out the race, and I'd
run the trusties; the dogs would go after them. I'd take them and
put them on his track. Sometimes the scent would be old. I have
run, put out a track this evening for about two miles and picked
the boy up—let him go to a certain tree and I'd track him.

Next to the dog yards is where I lived. I run the dogs for nine
years; I lived over there nine years.

Many times when I was running a escaped prisoner there
would be two of us on horseback—me and another prisoner.
He was the most trusted convict. Then there was two prisoners
with a dog apiece on a line. Those were the ones coming up
behind. That's 'cause they wouldn't run as fast as the dogs that
was loose.

We run one prisoner—a dog boy, too—we run that prisoner
'til I run the horse to death. That horse died that first twenty
miles.

That race was so fast. The dogs would make a loop and give a
horse a chance to catch its breath, but that dog boy just took a
beeline; he knowed where his home was, you know. He took just
a beeline towards home and the dogs didn't make a bobble, they
just went right on 'till they run that horse—it got so hot it just
failed.

That prisoner, he stayed away from water too. I run that prisoner 'til I run the horse to death; then the prisoner got a ride,
hired somebody to carry him home, and I knew where he lived,
so I knew where his sister lived and I knew where his mother
lived, too. Over there on the river. So, we run him to where a fella

said he'd picked him up and carried him home. So, I went to his sister's house first. She told me, says, "Mr. Dees, he's gone over to Momma's," and says, "now, I'll go over there and go in the house first if you won't shoot him if he runs out." I said, "I won't shoot him." I said, "I'll go to the back door, you'll know I'm at the back door, and if he comes out the back door I'll just catch him." And I says, "You go in the front, and this man here, another free man, Mr. Loreman, he'll go to the front door with you and I'll go to the back door."

And he had been there, him and another prisoner. They had been there and the mother had given them some quilts and things to sleep, and they went from there way back in the river swamp to a old house that was back there nobody lived in. And this sister of his told us that she'd go show us where they was at, which was about two miles we had to walk, through the woods, through the water and everything else. And she went with us over there to that house and called him and told him, says, "Mr. Dees is out here, wants to carry you back to the prison, now get up and get your stuff and come on out." So, he got up and got his quilts and all, come on out, him and the other prisoner, so we went on back to the house, to his mother's, and she was sitting on the front porch and she fainted when we walked up, so he asked me could he go in there where his momma was and I told him yeah, I let him go on in there just like he was a trusty. In other words, I turned him loose again!

That goes to show you, if you'll treat one fair, if he's got any man in him at all. 'Course the boy that shot me—there's just a whole lot of them over there like that. You could give them chicken and cake three times a day, and they'd tote a Bible under their arm 'til they wore it out and all that sort of stuff; they'd get a parole and just the time they got out they'd throw the Bible away and do something else and come back and pick up that same Bible—if they'd changed wardens, see—and go to trying to put that same hat on him! So, that's what you have to get up against.

One night, right here, I run three prisoners. Caught one of them—used to be a house set right there, caught one of them right out there. Brought him up and give him to a man that lived in this house. Run another right up yonder and caught him in a barn and the other one got away. About a week or two after then I caught the other one. They were trying to hide out in the trees here. They run across on foot and it's about fifteen miles from here to Atmore prison, right through these woods here.

Another time I run a prisoner down this paved road, right straight into Atmore and they told me I was crazy. I had one dog that was running 'cause I was afraid the cars would kill him, so I had it running right ahead of me and she—like when the prisoner would meet a car with the lights, he'd get out and lay down in the ditch—well, she'd get to where if he run out and lay down in the ditch, she'd go out there to where he laid down and bring him back into the road and go on down the road. And I run him right into Atmore and got him in the depot down there—caught him in the depot, and I run him right back by the prison; on the way into town, he come back by the prison! I run him up above the prison, about a mile (and it got dark) and then come right back by the prison! Doubled back. Trying to throw me off, and he would have thrown me off 'cause everybody thought I was crazy for following that dog. They told me, says, "You crazy." So, I followed that dog and I caught him.

There was another that robbed a man in Mississippi and he'd come over in Alabama; he'd robbed a man in Mississippi and kidnapped him and then come in Alabama and turned him loose, and then he'd rob and kidnap a man in Alabama and go back into Mississippi. So, I stayed down in Mobile a week with the dogs, and he didn't do anything while I was in Mobile 'cause they had it in the paper. And he said he wouldn't be took alive.

When I come back to Atmore, and it was in the paper that I had come back to Atmore, the next day he robbed another man in Alabama and carried him back in Mississippi. So, late that evening they run into him, some kids did, parked in a road way off in the woods, and they seen he was asleep. So they went back and told they folks about it and they called and got the law up there, and when they went in there on him he jumped out of the car and run and dropped his gun, but he had his belt full of cartridges. So they called me and I got down there—that happened about four o'clock that evening and I got down there about ten o'clock that night, put the dogs on his track and run him all night up to about nine o'clock the next morning—run him in a house and caught him. I asked him when I caught him, I said, "What would you have done if you had had that gun?" "I had a machine gun," he says, "I'd have made you melt the barrel off that machine gun." They sent him to the penitentiary for twenty-five years, I believe. He went to federal prison. He just gave up whenever he seen me.

I run one one night from the prison to Frisco City, which is twenty-two miles—I run him afoot! And lost him in Frisco City, come back to the prison and just about the time I got back to the prison they called and said he went up to a house and wanted some matches. And I went back up there and got after him again and I run him all day 'til three o'clock that evening, and I had got so tired 'til I'd get straddled of a fence and I couldn't get my legs over that fence. So I told the deputy warden that we would never catch him. I'd see some people that would tell me, "He's 'bout hour ahead of you, 'bout hour ahead of you, 'bout hour ahead of you." I couldn't gain on him and he couldn't gain on me! 'Course, I was running the dog on that line. 'Cause I was in a country where I was afraid I'd get some dogs killed if I turned them loose. So I told the deputy warden to call the prison on the radio and tell them to bring me some more dogs and a horse and I could catch the man in a few minutes. So, they brought me a horse and some more dogs and I dropped him, caught him in about thirty minutes. But, I run him, I run that prisoner at least forty miles. Most of it was on foot. That was back, let's see, that was back about '38, '38 or '39, way back.

Oh, yeah, I've lost them. I've lost them. Folks would pick them up on the road, but they don't pick up as many prisoners as you think. In other words, they wouldn't pick up as many prisoners then as they will now. 'Cause now you can't tell a prisoner from a free people. At that time trusties wore white clothes and line men wore stripes, stripes up and down their leg; and they finally got where they put white clothes on all of them, see. But now they wear these here twenty-five dollar navy slacks up there. Yes! You can't tell a prisoner now from a free man. In other words, the guards has got on a uniform now and the prisoners has got on street clothes! That's how much change has been made in it.

They put the guard in a uniform and put street clothes on the convict! They said somebody give them to them. But, still it don't make no difference if some manufacturer did give them to them, the prisoners didn't have no business with them. They need to be in a uniform where the public can tell whether he's a prisoner or not. And they ought to have numbers on them clothes big enough to show they are prisoners.

And your sentence didn't have a thing in the world to do with the penalty for escape. There was a boy that left Atmore that I went to school with, that just had a half day! He was a carpenter. He was the kind of prisoner we called a county prisoner. He was in there for a misdemeanor, over here in Atmore. He thought he had a hold on him, so he was out in the carpenter squad and he walked off. He had made his time, all but a half a day and he left and was gone for about six months—and one day at twelve o'clock he come walking back! Come walking up and I was at the front gate, and he says, "Captain Dees, I want to check back in and make that half a day, I found out I didn't have a hold-over." So we checked him out the next day and he worked that half a day. The next morning we turned him loose! At that time he had his time made and they'd either punish him by the strap or, well, that was mostly what they'd use was the strap then.

A hold-over is where a man is in the penitentiary and another charge has come up that they thought he was guilty of it, and a hold-over is where they will put an arrest record on his jacket and when he fills that sentence instead of him going out he has to go back to jail to be tried again.

I was against adding another sentence for escaping. If a man's got twenty-five or thirty-five or forty years, what'd he care about another year and a day? For running. If he gets away he's got all to gain and nothing to lose. If he gets away, okay. If they give him another year, it's still okay; he's got more time then he can make anyhow. So I didn't like that, and another thing I didn't like was to put that much burden on the taxpayers—to have to go through court and give that fellow some more time and take up the time of the courts and all that, when there wasn't no use to it.

What'd I do after training dogs? I got shot, you know. Then I

got a horse fell on me and ruptured me, and they had to operate
on me. That's when they sent me to Ketona to run that prison
up there.

I got shot in 1934. A prisoner took a gun from a guard and
shot me with a .38/.40 rifle. Came right near killing me, and I
stayed in the hospital for thirty-six days, I believe.

Soft-nosed bullet. I still got the bullet in me. If I hadn't stood
up in the saddle he would have killed me 'cause he would have
shot me through the chest. He shot me through the top part of
the hip.* At the time, I was running the dogs and he was a trusty,
a dog boy. A white boy, too, and I fed him off my own table. But
he had a criminal record. They had him for carnal knowledge
to start with. That was fooling with a girl under sixteen years
old. Well, then they got him for attempted rape. He made that
sentence, and they got him for attempted rape again and he made
that. All right, then they turned him out and then he got in the
penitentiary for rape and they gave him a life sentence.

----

*Fred Dees, Sr.: "Daddy couldn't get back up on the horse. He drug
himself about a mile and a half before they ever found him. Then they
loaded him in the car and brought him to the state farm. The convict
shot him pretty close to where he lives at now, over in that community
near Atmore. They drove all the way back to the state farm with him,
carried him in the back of an old car, and I went out to the window of
the car and seen him, and he had khaki clothes and his clothes was
bloodied all over; you couldn't see a spot on them that wasn't blood.
He'd done bled so much. He had passed out then. Then they carried
him to Atmore to the doctor, and hauled him all the way to Century,
Florida, about thirty miles, where there was a hospital. Which, now
the doctor seen him before he left the state farm—they had a doctor
there that stayed there, in other words he lived in a house—he was the
doctor for the convicts and he doctored all the personnel too. One of
those doctors that wore a cape.

"Daddy was running the convict then. After the convict shot him he
got the gun and picked it up and braced it on his clothes and said 'that's
for Dees.' Later, the sheriff caught him. They kept him for a long time.
During the time that Daddy was warden at Ketona in Birmingham,

Well, he shot me—we made a trusty out of him and all—and he shot me, and they give him another parole. In other words, he got some prisoner or another in there—we had prisoners in the office—he got them to do away with that record in there where he took a gun away from a guard and shot me with it; he had them do away with that record so it wouldn't show on his record in Montgomery! Well, the parole board paroled him! And I run into him in Birmingham and I thought he was out on escape, and he seen me and run. 'Course, he was scared; he was afraid I'd kill him, so he run. So I called up there to Montgomery and I asked if they let McCann out and they said, "Yeah, we paroled him." I says, "You mean you gave that prisoner a parole after he took a gun away from a guard and shot me with it!" And, Miz Marshall, she was the head of the parole board, she told me, she says, "Dees, it don't show on his record where he took a gun and shot you with it." I said, "Well, he sure did, and it's supposed to be on his record." Well, they got to checking and she called me back and told me, says, "I'll tell you what we'll do, we'll send and get him, have him picked up." I told them, I said, "No, just leave him out, if he'll do all right, that's all right with me." So, about a month after that they caught him in a tourist court with a twelve-year-old girl and both of them with their clothes off. So they brought him back, put him in the penitentiary, and just before I went back to Kilby he had a heart attack and died.

Oh, they'd escape all right. And you'd lose your job if you didn't shoot him. That was the rules. You'd also lose your job if you went to sleep on one of those towers up there where you was supposed to stay awake and watch around the perimeter of the

---

McCann made parole and Daddy was at the bus station one night for some reason or another, I don't remember, but anyway he seen McCann at the bus station and McCann run from him when he seen him. But then he broke his parole, and was put back in Kilby prison, and Daddy went back. He was laid off, you know, during that time, and when he went back, he went to work at Kilby prison. McCann was in the TB hospital then. He died in the prison TB hospital. It was about eight or nine years. He served about eight years after he shot Daddy before he got out, and Daddy ran into him at the bus station."

fence—see that nobody got out. They had a railroad steel out there, and they let you hit it, just like a clock striking. And if you missed one of them—the man at the front started it—Number One Tower, Number Two Tower, Number Three Tower, Number Four Tower, right on around, you'd follow it, right behind the other. Well, all right, if Number One Tower hit his, then Number Two didn't hit, they sent a guard around there and seen what was wrong with him. And if he was asleep, that was his job.

They paid fifteen dollars a head if a prisoner escaped and got away from us, they paid fifteen dollars. Not to us, no. I got paid just like a guard. Drawed a check just like a guard. After he got away from us and somebody happened to see him and catch him, they'd pay him fifteen dollars for catching him. Now, you wouldn't pay if they just told you where he was at, 'cause you went and got him. Sometimes the warden would pay them, but it'd just be goodness in him.

Now, I shot one when I first went there to work. He run out of an uncle of mine's squad and I shot him. Ninety-seven steps. And I shot him down. 'Course he died after then. And he was in there for stealing chairs out of a nigger church!

That was the only prisoner I had to run away from me. He run from my uncle, my mother's brother, and I shot him. I shot him, he was ninety-seven steps from where I was standing to where he fell. But, he run from my mother's brother. I shot him. I was carrying a sports gun, a shotgun. Double aught buckshot. I shot over him the first time and hollered for him to stop and he didn't stop—and I hadn't been working there but just a little while—and there was an ol' guard pretty close to me—he was too far to shoot him, so he hollered and told me, says, "All right, Dees, if you're going to do anything, you better do it," so I had an ol' shotgun that belonged to me that I was using that had hammers on it, so I cocked the other barrel and I shot him. He fell just like that. 'Course, they got over there to take the shot out of him.

There was a bunch of guards there with me, and we was digging up stumps off the farm, cleaning up that farm you see out there. There was forty men pretty close to where I was at.

I actually brought him in, out in the field, digging stumps. I heard him when he dropped the shovel, and I turned around and he was running and I hollered for him to stop—he was running from one of Momma's brothers. 'Course there wasn't no way in the world for my uncle to shoot, so I ordered him to stop and he didn't pay no attention to me and so I shot over him and hollered for him to stop again; he didn't stop, then I shot him. I killed that fella, I was over on that other hill, right yonder, on that little rise, right over yonder, digging stumps. And, he run across thisaway, and he had crossed that ditch down there at the bottom and was coming up this hill on this side and I was over on the other side and I shot him. Ninety-seven steps. Ninety-seven steps.

They took him over there to the prison and took him to the hospital and a doctor in Atmore. Dr. Weber was the doctor then, and he come out and examined him and all and he said the shot worked out of his back when he was moving around there; they dropped back out of his back. Well, I didn't think they did, but two, three days after then his fever run up high and they carried him to Atmore and took X-ray pictures and one of them shots went in his kidney, and he set up blood poisoning and blood poisoning killed him. The shot didn't kill him. If they would have took him on down there that evening and took a X-ray picture and found the shot, cut in there and got it, the man would probably be living today.

At that time they had a rule, if you didn't shoot him, you lost your job. Now, we used to work all that land up through that bottom, we worked it all. Everything was cleaned up; you could see if a man run away up yonder, you could get out here and see him coming across there. In other words, they just wouldn't run 'cause you could see them too far.

There was one time while I was dog warden, there was one whole year that I didn't have but thirteen men to run, and I caught twelve of them. And we had 'round seventeen-hundred men then. I don't think they have too many to run today 'cause they keep them all shut up. A ten-year-old boy could keep them shut up. But put them out here and work them in these fields, they got to have some men that'll stay on the job and watch them or they'll lose a whole lot of them. They'll lose more than thirteen a year 'cause they'd have more than that in trusties walk off, I imagine.

I mentioned the mother gave her son quilts and things? Well, a mother will do anything for her son—that's love that naturally is there. I've seen mothers come and give boys money—the last penny they had—probably they didn't have nothing to eat when they got home; before they could get outside the prison they'd be lost that money for buying some dope or another or this here sexual stuff that they—sex perverts—that they'd spend it that way or something and use the last nickel that they had.

Well, one day I had a mother and a father, I never would hold nothing from a mother and a father. That's the hardest thing to do, that is. One of the hardest things to do in the prison is to tell a mother and a father a lie, and I just naturally wouldn't do it. And he—how sorry the boy is—well, they come in my office, I was at Kilby, they come in the office and they say, "Something has happened to my boy since he's been in the penitentiary, he's changed." Well, I knew that he was a sex pervert, a homosexual. He was, if you want to make it like it is, he was the girl. So I told his mother, I says, "You go on out and I'll tell your husband what's wrong with your boy, then he can tell you. I won't tell you, I'll tell him and he can tell you."

Well, I told this boy's father, and his father cried and he says, "Mr. Dees, I knew that there was something wrong with my boy, he ain't the same boy that he was when he come in." But I never did keep nothing away from the parents; I told them if he was a, if he wasn't any 'count, I'd tell them. I says, "That boy's not worth the powder and shot it would take to kill him." And I told one mother one time, I says, "When you, when this boy was born you'd been better off if you'd just pulled his head off and throwed him in a trash can. You would have saved a whole lot of pains in heart and a whole lot of trouble and a whole lot of money, and he won't never be one worth a nickel to you. To him or nobody else." That's bad to say to a mother, but I says, "I'm just telling you now when you give birth to him, if you'd just pulled his head off and throwed him in a trash can you'd been better off and everybody else would have been better off." And they would of. He was one of the sorriest prisoners that I ever did see.

All your troubles in a penitentiary is mostly about gal boys. They kill—90 percent of your killings in the penitentiary is over that. Your gal boys sells himself. They'll go to the table to eat

together, and say they wouldn't give them—generally on Sunday they'd give them a piece of steak or pork chop or a piece of
chicken or something like that—they wouldn't give them all they
could eat, they'd just give them one piece. Well, the tush hog
would give his gal boy his piece of chicken or his pie or his extra,
or whatever it was.
     Tush hog is a man that's has got his gal boy. That's a tough—
he's tough. 'Gator. That's a nickname for the same as 'gator. A
'gator is one that really don't take no junk off nobody. He's an
individual by himself; he goes for bad. But, now a tush hog, he's
got his wife. That's convicts' slang.
     As long as a man could keep his wife straight I just let it álone!
In other words, if he got to running over a prisoner or mistreating
him some way or another, I'd step in and get him straight, but if
he just wanted to live like that and wanted to do things like that,
okay, there wasn't nobody making him do it, that was left up to
him, so I didn't do nothing about it.
     One time we locked all the gal boys up to where they separated
them from the rest of them. We done it! We made them make
us a cell, put all the gal boys in it and put the men in the other
cells. We couldn't do nothing with them gal boys, they tore up
all our plumbing, tore up all the beds and everything else! We
couldn't do a thing in the world with them. We fed them separate
and everything and come to find out—well, they do it in the
street, so when they get in there, they'll do it in there. We found
out it was better to let them run loose 'cause their husband would
keep the wife straight sort of like it do in the free world! They
could handle them better by mixing them up than they could by
trying to separate them. People are funny, you can't tell about
people.*

---

*Fred Dees, Sr.: "In the road camps we would have that problem. We
didn't have as much in the road camps 'cause we didn't have as many
prisoners. But when we come up with that situation we would for punishment to stop it, as much as we could, we would dress the woman up
in woman's clothes and handcuff them together on visiting Sunday
and let all visitors see them. And that discouraged a lot of that."

And they doing something now that we've always done—we've tried it two, three times, it won't work—they're doing it now, and I hope it works for them, but I can't see where it's going to work. They're building a trusty barracks on the outside of the prison, going to put trusties out there; well the trusties are going to slip off to some women or another somewhere (which you can't hardly blame them) and all that sort of stuff.

There's no supervision out there; if it's supervised then they just as well put a cell in the prison and just call it a trusty cell—put all the trusties in there and they won't have to have but one bunch of supervision where they're going to have two bunches of supervision, run two kitchens and all that sort of stuff.

Where the road camps had it over us they would let their wives visit them. We didn't have the facilities for that, which you couldn't hardly start it in a prison nohow 'cause they'd be claiming it was his wife and it wasn't his wife. First thing you know you'd be letting somebody's women folks in there and cause some trouble. You couldn't afford to do it in a prison. The road camps you could. Most of the time they try to send a prisoner as close to his home as they could. In one way it's all right, and in one way it's not. 'Cause you liable to let a man's daughter in there that claims she's some prisoner's wife or another and she comes up pregnant and that man sues the state of Alabama for no telling what. So you can't do no such stuff as that there's much less—in other words as long as it's colored it's all right, but . . .

The reason I got suspended had to do with escapes. When we could, we used informers. In this case, I was told to give some canned goods from the prison to a woman for payment, which I did. Well, later they said, "We're going to charge you with using state property for your personal use and fifty dollars will get the thing satisfied," but that was after my suspension. I was suspended right close to a year. Close to a year, I was suspended that long. And I was warden at Ketona then.

What did I do that whole year? I run a store—I bought a little ol' grocery store down here, right here at the end of Green Street in Atmore. Me and the wife had between nine thousand and ten

thousand dollars and I come down here and bought that little
ol' grocery store and I'd sell stuff on credit and I was eating white
meat and baloney sausage and wieners and everything else trying
to make ends meet. And folks was buying T-bone steaks and
center-cut ham and all that sort of stuff, sitting on the front row
of the church, and they just eat up that between nine thousand
and ten thousand dollars, and on top of that they eat up two thousand dollars that Momma had, that I borrowed from her.

So when I got all this thing settled, went back to work for the
state, I got a lawyer there at Evergreen, he's dead now, got him
to open it up every Saturday and sell it. I went and took inventory
and I had enough stuff in there to pay off all the bills I owed,
and so I opened it up every Saturday and sold it at cost and paid
off my bills and all that sort of stuff. I give him the books and
all and so I went back to work for the state and he settled the thing
up—but I got enough money out of it to pay Momma and my
brother their money back. I done that the night that I closed,
and my money—there's two fellas joined the Holiest Church,
one of them owed me three dollars and something and one of
them owed me four dollars and something—well, if you belong
to the Holiest Church you got to pay your debt, so they sent me
the money. That's all the money I got out. The other people
never did pay—no, they never did pay.

I paid my fifty-dollar fine, I did, and come on back, and I went
with the director up there and they put me back to work. But
they wouldn't pay me for my back time 'cause I paid my fine.

It didn't bother my work record 'cause I didn't bother my
retirement or nothing like that. I left all my retirement money
just like I left it, then whenever I went back to work I picked it
right back up. Whole lot of folks draws their retirement out if
something happens to them, but I didn't draw my retirement
out. So when I went back to work I picked it up right where I left
off and that's how come I draw as much as I draw today.

I went back to work at Kilby and I had to borrow money—I
had to borrow the money to move to Kilby. And I went back to
work for the state and stayed there then until I retired. That's all
the trouble I had, and all the work that I done with the state that's

all the time that I was off during the whole thirty-eight years—
and I was doing what the boss told me to do then!*

After I got away from Ketona, which was in Birmingham, and
got down to Kilby, that's all they wanted was to get me away from
up there. As long as I was there I run my business and let them
run theirs, and I wouldn't let them interfere with my business
and I wouldn't interfere with theirs.

Just like the morning the snow was all over the ground and it
was cold and the prisoners didn't have good clothes—they didn't
have wool clothes, they didn't have nothing but cotton clothes;
and in the case of an emergency it would have been all right, I'd
have made arrangements to go out there and open the highway,
or something like that, if the traffic could have got blocked or
something that away; but just ordinarily they want to check the
men out, and I told them that I wouldn't let them have them
'cause it was too cold, a man couldn't work out there with them
cotton clothes on, and I wasn't going to put a prisoner out there
to do something that I couldn't do.

This was still at Ketona, which consisted of about a hundred-
fifty to two-hundred-fifty men and women. So, they had two
prisons in Jefferson County, two just alike, one in the north end
of the county and one in the south end of the county—that's the
county Birmingham's in—so I called the fellas and told them
what I'd done, I also told the commissioner, the one I was having
the trouble with, I told him, I says, "Now you got a good overcoat,
if you'll go out and stand in front of the courthouse thirty minutes
with the best clothes that you've got, you've got a good wool suit

---

*Fred Dees, Sr.: "He stayed laid off a year, so he had to go back, let's
see, I went to work for the state in '52, so he had to go back, it must have
been '50 when he got laid off then he went back to work in '51 'cause
he had, he was already deputy warden at Kilby in '52, August of '52,
when I went to work, which it didn't take him but about six months to
go from guard to deputy warden when he went back to work. He hired
back in as a guard, then he went to captain of the guard, then he went
to deputy warden. That's the policy."

on and an overcoat, you go out there and stand there in that cold
thirty minutes and come back in there and call me and tell me a
man can work out there in that cold weather, I'll check these
men out." He says, "No, I ain't going out there and stand in no
cold weather." I says, "Okay, I'm not going to check these men
out unless it's an emergency, even if they are prisoners, I'm not
going to check them out." So he got mad about that. My boss at
Montgomery then put me over both camps 'cause the other man
had checked the men out, he checked his men out in that cold
weather. So then he put me over both camps; if the weather's
too bad for my men to work I called him and told him that I didn't
want him to check his out either.

The men were working on the roads—all together. They
paid us so much a month, I mean, yeah, so much a month for the
prisoners, and we took them and took care of them and everything. The county would rent them from the state. When the
men couldn't work I'd just have to leave them inside where it was
warm 'cause I didn't have a yard to turn them in, but if it was too
cold to work they wouldn't be out in no yard, they'd be in the
cell blocks. They could play cards or dominoes or whatever they
wanted to do inside the building. 'Course I just had misdemean-
ors up there; I didn't have no hard criminals. That was Ketona,
but it was a state prison. Medium security. We had supervision
over them.

Now, we had some really tough prisoners, but I never had
none I couldn't handle, at any prison. They got some over at
Atmore now they can't handle. 'Course, they can be handled if
they had the right man over there to handle them. There's prisoners over there that's done everything in the book; there ain't
nothing—there's some prisoners over there that's done everything mentionable. Anything that a man can do, they've done it.

I stayed in it thirty-eight years and I know one thing: you got
to have strict discipline if you run that prison over there. Discipline number one. Security number two. Discipline. The Bible
speaks of discipline all the way through it. Discipline. And whenever you get away from the Bible, you done got away from it all.

If they'd run that prison up there at Atmore according to the Bible—it says use the rod, don't spare the rod—it doesn't say nothing about no strap, but it says something about that rod, and that rod can be used as a strap or an oak limb or whatever you want to call it! But it means getting a man under control, see.

It goes back to the fella that had a mule that wouldn't do right at all; he just couldn't do a thing in the world with him. So he told his neighbor, says, "I got to do something with this mule, I can't do nothing with this mule," and the neighbor told, says, "Mr. Jones down the road there is a good, good man to train a mule, he could really train a mule." So he went down to see Mr. Jones and Mr. Jones told him, "I'll be up there in the morning." So he come walking up there the next morning, he had an ax handle in his hand and he says, "Where's that mule?" He says, "There he is right out there." Says, "Run him in that stall." They run him in the stall. He shut the door and he got in there and he just begin to beat that ol' mule good and proper, see, and the man opened the door and says, "Hey there, Mr. Jones, you going to kill my mule! What've you done?" "Well," says Mr. Jones, "the first thing I got to do is get his attention." Well, if you don't get their attention and don't keep their attention you hadn't got no prisoners.

A strap is about six-feet long, and the end that they use to hit the man with has got about, oh, I'd say eighteen inches, it's just a strap about three-inches wide; it's just like a razor strap. Now it tapers from that eighteen inches up to the handle where you, the man that uses it, a piece of leather on each side of it the width of the leather that they use at the tip, and it makes it stiffer up there to where he can control it. In other words, if it didn't have some support in it, you couldn't control it; you're liable to hit a man back of the head, you're liable to hit them on his feet or anywhere.

The strap was used when a man committed a crime—say he cut another prisoner, they found him with a knife, or he quit work or murdered another prisoner or something like that. They could give him twenty-one lashes, but that's all they could give him, and that had to be in the presence of a doctor, and the doctor had to examine him before it was administered and all that sort of stuff. And the doctor sit there all the time that you hit him, and you had to hit him on the buttocks; you couldn't hit him no where else. You couldn't hit him up on his kidneys or anywhere like that, you had to hit him on the buttocks. And sometimes they wouldn't give him but three licks and the prisoner would say, "I'll do better if you'll just quit."

Which, I think, that's the most humane punishment there is. 'Cause this here putting them in solitary, locking them up in a place and leaving him there for so many days is a whole lot worse than just taking him in and spanking him a little bit—that's the end of it. And you can't say—some folks will say if a man was to give me a spanking with a strap I'd kill him. Well, that's all bull. There's nobody punished no more prisoners than I have, and I've never met a prisoner on the street that he wasn't glad to see me! And always come over to shook hands with me and all that sort of stuff. Which, I tried to be fair, I tried to be to where a man knowed I knew he was to be guilty before I punished him, and then I punished him and I didn't hold nothing against him; I'd do as much for him as I would before I had ever done anything.

In order to use the strap you'd write up to the director and tell him what this prisoner had done, and tell him that you wanted the order to give him so many straps, lashes; then the director then would write you back and give you permission to whup him. Well, all right, twenty-one licks is all you can hit him, that is the law. And there was a doctor who stood there and examined him 'fore he was punished, and he examined him after he was punished, and the warden was there, the doctor was there, the deputy was there and whoever—in other words there was always three or four or five in there—then whenever you got through with it, it was written on that sheet, if you didn't give him but three licks—a whole lot of times three licks you could tell the prisoner was a changed prisoner. Right then, that's the time to quit. You can tell when he's come under and if you hadn't give him but three licks, it's just write it on that order that you just gave the man three licks. And the doctor would sign it, the man's in good shape, physically and every way.

But, at the time they threw that strap away it was nothing but bread and water. A man could stay in the doghouse, say, twenty days, and he would lose—a man your size, kind of skinny—would lose six inches in the waist. If he was sick, the doctor examined him every day. The doctor examined him every day, and if he was sick in there, he took him out and put him in the hospital. Then whenever he got well they'd put him back in there until he'd finished his time.

The doghouse, it's about a five by eight. That's solitary confinement. And it hasn't got any windows in it. It's dark in there and it's got a fan on top that runs and circulates air through it all the time, and you can't see out of it—it's dark. Like I say there's no danger in it at all, the fan's running, circulating air in it; it's got central heat in it just like the prison's got. There's no way for a man to freeze to death in there if he's in there without any clothes. I've put one prisoner in there without any clothes.

We got a floor in there for a toilet in the bottom of it, in the floor—just a hole in the floor. You put a toilet in there and they'd just tear it up. You flushed it from the outside—the guards flushed it. They flushed it about four times every twenty-four hours. That's what it was. Oh, if somebody, some guard, went in there for some reason or another to pick one up that—you could hear them hollering, tell you they was sick in there—the guards would go in there and see about it, then they'd go three times a day to feed them, then they'd go between time to wash, they watered them six times a day and they fed them three times a day. So, naturally, if there was anything in there that was wrong, the guards would know.

I don't imagine they'd get very hot in there. Or very cold either, 'cause you take a place that's got a breeze coming through it—now I didn't stay in there, I don't know how hot it would get—but the more men you had in there the heat from their bodies would make them hot. If you just had one man in there, I imagine he'd get cold, but if you had three, four, five men in there then their bodies would keep the place warm, see.

That's what they got punished with, and it ain't enough to handle some of them. To handle one class of them, yeah, but to handle another class of them, no.

You could put him there for twenty-one days. And the doctor goes in there every day and checks them.*

Now, twenty-one days in that doghouse will actually hurt your health. Now, spanking your fanny won't hurt your health. It'll heal. It won't hurt you, it'll hurt your feelings. It takes one of them to hurt your health, the other one takes the pride out of you. You'd hate to get your fanny whupped. And you'd do anything you can from getting it spanked so your friends and your family wouldn't know it. So that's the reason I argue that the strap is the best, 'cause the solitary confinement will really hurt your health and the strap won't hurt your health.**

----

*Fred Dees, Sr.: "That was the amazing thing to me, they could whup him, give him twenty-one licks; done away with that and come around with the doghouse or solitary confinement and set it up just like a strap. Twenty-one days. It'll kill you."

**From the weekly Atmore *Advance*, March 27, 1975: "In two separate cases last week, the 5th U.S. Circuit Court of Appeals in New Orleans found that a Fountain Correctional Center (formerly Atmore State Prison) guard did not impose cruel and inhuman punishment by using tear gas after a prisoner threw a cup of urine in his face, but the court ruled that isolation cells in Alabama's prisons are so bad that they constitute cruel and unusual punishment.

"In the latter decision, the court called for an overhaul of the lockup units commonly referred to as 'the doghouse.'

"In making the decision the court overturned a decision by Judge Brevard Hand of Mobile that isolation was within the law.

"The New Orleans court, in overturning Hand, described one cell like this:

" 'As many as seven of them are placed in a cell which measures six feet by eight feet. These cells are essentially concrete boxes with no bunks, toilets, sinks or other facilities. A hole in the cell floor serves as a toilet. This is flushed four times per day by a guard who has access to the flushing mechanism. Flushing frequently causes the waste to back up onto the floor of the cell. Inmates placed in punitive isolation live in these conditions day and night for as long as 21 days.'

"The court ordered Hand to enter 'an appropriate injunctive order' to end such conditions.

And another thing, when a man does a crime, or breaks a rule,
he needs punishing then, right then, while it's on his mind, while
he's got hell in him, right then's the time to get it out of him. In
three, four days, by the time you write to Montgomery and get
an order and put him in the doghouse, or give him a trial—now
you got to have the judge and everything else over there to give
him a trial, and he can get him a lawyer and all that sort of stuff.
They ought to have several different types of punishment
for different types of offenses. You just say, "All right I'm going
to use the strap on everybody that breaks the rules," well, I'd be
against that. 'Cause you can take five boys in the same family,
the same brothers and sisters—I mean brothers—all of them
have the same mother and father, they'll be two in that bunch
won't never give no trouble. All right, there'll be two in that bunch
that you can talk to and get them to do anything you want to, and
there'll be one in that same bunch that you couldn't get him to
do nothing right! You've seen it yourself in everyday life. So
that's the same thing over there, exactly. It ain't a thing in the
world but a family of boys, is what it is.

"This case was brought by Holman inmate Robert McCray and Fountain inmates Jerry White and Alvin Clayborne.

"The 5th Circuit Court also ordered Hand to hold hearings on whether
homosexuals should be separated from other inmates. McCray claimed
that homosexuals pose a serious security threat to the other prisoners.

"In the decision involving the guard, the court ruled that the guard,
identified only as Officer Greggs, was justified in using tear gas to stop
a disturbance at the prison. Inmate Johnny Clemmons brought the
suit against the guard for damages.

"The incident happened on July 16, 1972, while three guards were
making a head count. The prisoners began cursing the guards and
then threw liquid and solid objects at them, the court said.

"One of the canisters of tear gas used to stop the disturbance landed
in front of Clemmons' cell and was left there for 30 minutes.

"After the incident the guard was punished by prison officials because they thought the use of tear gas was excessive. The guard was
suspended for one week without pay."

An example of what a prisoner would do to deserve punishment? Well, if he got out of hand and if you had a rule—a warden
over there at the prison has got to set him up some rules—and
put that in the prison where all the prisoners will know what to
do and what not to do, let them know that. All right, then if they
do it, if they haul off and take your money away from you, then
punish them. If he kills another prisoner, punish him. In other
words, he ought to be electrocuted. But, you see the Supreme
Court's done away with the chair.* Once it was automatically
death if he killed a guard; he was automatically sent to the chair.
If he killed another inmate, that would be left up to the jury and
'course it would all be left up to the jury, but if he killed a free
man he'd sure get the chair. 'Course, kill another inmate, it would
be all depend on how he killed him and what he killed him for

---

*From the *Advance* for September 4, 1975: "Judge Johnson [U.S. District Court Judge Frank M. Johnson Jr.] issued an order requiring the
state to improve conditions in the isolation and segregation units at all
prisons. He said that by noon on Wednesday, Sept. 3, all isolation and
segregation cells must have toilets that flush from inside the cells, mattresses for inmates to sleep on, and proper lighting. Also, inmates must
be served three meals a day instead of just one.

"Capps [Associate Prison Commissioner Walter Capps, serving as
acting warden of Holman Prison and Fountain Correctional Center]
said Wednesday morning that the segregation units at Holman and
Fountain were ready to meet the court standards. The isolation units
at Fountain and Holman have not been used for more than six months
so remodeling there did not have to be completed yesterday."

From an Associated Press wire story dated September 10, 1975:
"Montgomery, Ala.—Saying 'I hope we'll see some electrocutions in
this state,' Governor George C. Wallace signed into law yesterday a
bill restoring the death penalty in Alabama.

"'I hope this bill is upheld because there are some bad folks, black
and white, that ought to be electrocuted in this state,' Wallace said at a
news conference."

On July 2, 1976, the U.S. Supreme Court ruled that a law carrying
a mandatory death penalty for inmates convicted of murder while
serving a life sentence may not be unconstitutional. The decision did
not refer specifically to Alabama, but Alabama does have such a law.

The house in which Oscar Dees lived with his family while he was "dog warden" (caring for the dogs used in running down escaped convicts) at Atmore Prison Farm.

A dog pen at Atmore.

A SECTION OF HOLMAN PRISON NEAR ATMORE, ALABAMA.

A WINDOWLESS BUILDING FORMERLY USED AS A "DOGHOUSE" AT LOXLEY ROAD CAMP. ARTICLES NOW STREWN ABOUT THE BUILDING BELONG TO THE STATE HIGHWAY DEPARTMENT.

and all that sort of stuff, 'cause some of them that I know of that done things to other prisoners that—really, I wouldn't of blamed the prisoner if he killed him.

Now, you've got a certain amount of certain convicts that likes discipline. Oh, 90 percent of them like discipline! All the prisoners that's trying to do right and get out, they like strict discipline. The only ones that's fussing is the ones that wants to run over the other ones.

Another reason a convict wants—a certain percent of them—wants discipline is to where he can feel at ease, and build his time, too. That was one of the things the prisoners always praised me for was 'cause they could lay down and sleep at night and know them gangs wasn't going to come down there and bother them—'cause they knew I was going to take care of it if they did, and somebody would tell me about it and I'd see about it.

When I went to Kilby they had, we called them, gangs—there's a little bunch of them would run together and take money off of other prisoners and all that sort of stuff, rob the stores and what have you, and *that* Kilby was just as bad as it had ever been. So I had to handle it, sort of ease the dead wood on the men that was doing it; then I really got their attention, and I stayed there nine years and I didn't have a killing and I didn't have a man cut and I think that would be a good record right there.

And I fixed it to where a prisoner could go to bed and lay his stuff down on the other bed and they didn't bother it, and they could come up there and tell me so and so's got dope, wheres he got it, and I could go get it, and they'd tell me, "Mr. Dees, you got a good many knives back there," and they'd tell me who's got them; and I'd take a box down there, put it down in the cell, and tell them that I wanted all the knives put in that box—I didn't care who had them I just wanted them put in that box, and if I caught one after this time was out, that I was going to punish him. I'd go back in that length of time—if I give them an hour to put them in there—I'd go back in an hour and get the box and generally it was full of knives and I didn't hear any more about no knives for a long time. That's the way I kept my knives out of the prison.

And it boils down to that you got one class that you can talk to—there's one class that ain't going to give you no trouble at all, won't never give you no trouble. There's one class that's just a little bit mischievious, they'll give you a little trouble; you can talk to them and get them straight. Then there's another class that you might have to use some little ol' amount of discipline on. But there's one class of prisoners over there that I would say the strap is the only salvation for it. And you can't tell me it don't help a man forty or fifty years old, 'cause I have spanked men forty and fifty years old and they never did give no more trouble, and I'd meet them on the street [and] some of them would say if my daddy had a done that to me I never would have been in the penitentiary; and they didn't hold nothing against you—all of them have always been glad to see me, I've always shook hands with them and been nice to them.

So I just don't agree with them [the Board of Corrections]; I think they're doing one of the worst things that ever has been done—to let prisoners run the prison. And these here psychologists and criminologists, all them sort of people, they're all right for crazy people, if there's something wrong with his mind for them to talk to; but them folks over yonder—'course, I agree that all of them has got a loose screw in them, there's something wrong with every man over there, it might be stealing—he can't help it if he's just got to steal something—might be fighting, it might be robbing; stealing generally runs on. When he starts to stealing he'll finally wind up as robbing, and fighting generally winds up as murders and things like that—but I think in sex crimes he's out of balance some way or another that would make him want to rape somebody or anything like that. There's something wrong with the man and the Lord fixed him thataway, and there ain't no psychologist or criminologist or money or nothing else going to change what the Lord done. When he was born, he was born thataway, and when he dies he's going to die thataway. His records over there will prove it. 'Cause if he starts off getting in the penitentiary for petty larceny, he'll wind up in there for robbery or something. He's going to keep doing it.

Now, the man that comes in there and goes out and stay out, is a man who's temper got him in there. Probably some little ol' something happened to him and he got in there accidentally, some way or another. Well, them kinds of fellas won't never come back. You can parole them the next day and they won't come back. And I think that a whole lot of prisoners wouldn't come back. If they'd bring a young boy in, say a teen-age boy, sixteen or seventeen years old, bring him in the prison today, turn him in the prison with all that bunch and let him stay in there overnight, in the morning bring him up to the office, hit him twenty-one licks with the strap, turn him loose—he won't never come back. I think that would work in 95 percent out of the *young* boys. That's something that he ain't never had, is somebody to give him a good spanking and that'll let him know that he ain't no 'gator and he ain't going to have things like he wants it. Just give him a good spanking, tell him now, say, "If you come back in here, this is what you're going to get." And he'll go out and behave himself, I believe.

If the inmates wanted to discipline themselves, then they would do it, I suspect, but they'd get killed. That bunch that I'm talking about that wants to run the thing, that has took on the outside whatever they wanted and done whatever they wanted to do on the outside and papa and momma didn't correct them—run and got them out of jail every time he violated the law and bring him home and wouldn't punish him or nothing or wouldn't do nothing about it—well they not doing nothing. That's just like a patch of corn out there; you're just throwing fertilizer on it and expecting it to kill it and that makes it grow worser. In other words, call it you just throwing gas on the fire. That's exactly what you done.

Now, if papa went up there and got him out of jail and brought him home and took him out there behind that barn and got his attention, well then probably he wouldn't have to go back up there and get him no more. But that don't happen. He comes home and momma she takes him under her arm and say, "Poor son, they done you wrong, they ought not to have done you thataway." But if your momma told you, says, "Now don't you go out there and do so and so," and you went and done it, what did she do? She got on your fanny, didn't she? Well, that's what I'm talking about over there, same thing. And if you haven't got it, you haven't got anything. If Jennie Lee tells Freddy, says, "Now

Freddy, you can't go do so and so," and she tells Fred, and he says "I'm going to do it, I don't care what you all say," and they let him go on and do it, they've done that kid an unjust. That's what I'm talking about, right there. You go home, wherever you come from, and you can go down the street and everywhere you find a family that's got discipline, the children do what their parents say do, you'll see a good home. You see a family where the children tell their mother and father what to do, you won't see no home. You understand what I'm talking about? That's the same way with the prison, or it don't mean prison, church or anything else—policemen, if the people of Atmore haven't got respect for the police department, there ain't no use in having a police department down there! Discipline is something that works everywhere; everything through life is discipline.

Like I was saying before, when I first went to Kilby they had them little gangs out there in the back, and I'd been there about three days and I walked down in the white cell block and this here Harold Lighter, he was one of Jimmy Isle's buddies, he told me, he says, "Mr. Dees, now let me tell you something. You been running all the prisons you been in contact with, all the prisons you ever worked at, but I want to tell you now, this Kilby's different, you not going to run this prison." Well, no more he got it out of his mouth, I hung this cane and a twelve* in the seat of his britches and I kicked him flat over a water fountain and I reached, got him by the collar, and I carried him out and put him down in that doghouse and went back up there and told the warden what happened. I wrote a report up on him and I never did have no more trouble out of him.

It all boils down to when they know you mean business, that's all you have to do. If they know that you mean that they're not going to run it, that's it. You won't have no trouble in the prison. It's just as easy to run a prison as if you was to run a home and everybody was to understand that they have got to do right, that

---

*Fred Dees, Sr.: "The saying of the convict will tell you was that Daddy was the only man that could kick and hit at the same time."

you're not going to put up with this here "who shot John" stuff—
that's all you have to do. When you get that on their mind, your
trouble's over with.

Well, I don't think they took it that I was a bully or anything
like that. They just took it that I meant what I said. If I told a
prisoner, "You're going to do this," and it was wrong, I'd tell the
boss, I'd say, "That prisoner done what I said do; if you got anything to say about it, you get on me—he done what I said to do."
Well, they knew I'd do that, see, so they didn't mind doing what
I said to do 'cause they knew I'd back them up. So I never did have
no trouble with no prisoners.

I only had one prisoner threaten my life. I had one to call up
one time to tell the warden to tell me that he was going to kill me.
So the warden called me in there and told me, and I told him, I
says, "Well, if he was going to kill me he never would have called
you and told you he was going to kill me." I says, "He'd just killed
me and that's be it." Warden asked me, "Don't it bother you?" I
said, "No, it don't bother me. Just like I say, if he was going to kill
me he sure wouldn't told nobody nothing about it." Never did
see him.

On the other hand there's a whole lot that comes to see me,
but I'd have to go back, I think Simpson—Simpson was a bookkeeper of mine at Ketona, and him and his wife, his wife lived in
Georgia and he lived in, he was in the penitentiary, and I don't
think he had but five years, I believe, for forgery, and he took
heart trouble, and he had at home a rifle and some fishing tackle
and some things. I love to fish and hunt and stuff, and he made a
request through his wife and to his daughter if anything happened to him, he wanted me to have, well, his Kodak—I got it
in there now—his Kodak, his rifle, and his fishing tackle. He
requested them to give them to me and they give them to me
whenever he died. He died at my prison at Ketona. He was a good
prisoner.

I never have seen a prisoner yet that's been in prison under
me that wasn't glad to see me. Come all the way across the street
to shake hands with me. I never have had one that acted like he
resented it any at all, and I reckon I punished more prisoners

than anybody in the state. It's like I said before, I tried my best
to be right, I tried my best to be sure that the prisoner was guilty
before I punished him. Then when I punished him I forgot it,
just like he was my own young one. So they don't resent it, or they
haven't resented me; they've all spoke mighty well of me. They'd
say, "One thing about Mr. Dees, he'll punish you if you do something wrong, but he forgets it. He'll do you a favor if he can."
   I want to tell you what happened to me one time. This is really
funny. I was warden at a road camp, same road camp I was warden for nine years and didn't get but two disciplinary reports. I
went down, I was getting the county prisoners out of the jail in
Birmingham and carrying them out and putting them in the
prison and we was renting them to the county just like we was to
the Highway Department. So I went down and got this prisoner,
and he was from the north, and them fellas there in the jail they
was waiting for me to come for they knew I was going to come
with some sort of ol' junk. So he come out, he had enough pencils
to run the University of Alabama, writing paper and first one
junk then another, and a brief case.
   Oh, he was really fixed up. Dressed all up and I says, "Hey
there, boy," I says (he's a colored boy), I says, "Now where you're
going you ain't going to need them pencils and all that paper and
stuff." I says, "The best thing for you to do is send that stuff back
home." He says, "No, I might want to do a little writing." And I
says, "Well, that writing is liable to cause you a whole lot of trouble." He talked about it out of one side of his mouth; he was from
around Cleveland, Ohio, or somewheres.
   So I got him out to the prison. I decided that the best thing for
me to do before he got in there and started some agitating and
got my prisoners all messed up and everything—I had a good
prison—before he's start a whole lot of junk, be a penitentiary
lawyer—that's what we called them, penitentiary lawyers, see.
So I told him, "Before I put you back there and let you ruin about
half my prisoners, I suspect I'd better make a good south Alabama nigger out of you." So, I took his briefrase and all his pencils, all of his writing materials, and all that sort of stuff; I got
that strap out and I hit him about two times, let him know what
that was, carried him on back and put him in the cell. I don't know

what happened, but somebody told it in Montgomery that I got this boy's attention. So they sent and got him.

I must not have got all his pencils, no! So they take him down there to Montgomery and they made a trusty out of him, put him to driving for one of the fellas that went around and looked at all the road camps and all. And I often think about this; he'd eat at my prison, he'd come there driving whoever it was—I think it was Floyd Neighbors—he'd come there driving whoever inspected the prison; he never come there but what I'd always fix him a good dinner and all, which I let him eat with the officers and all that sort of stuff, and he'd always tell what I'd done.

And that goes to show you that they got respect for you if you get his. In other words, they got respect for you if you make them have respect for you. If you put yourself in the same class as him, if you put yourself on the same equal he is, he ain't got no respect for you. When he hasn't got any respect for you, you haven't got anything. This prisoner was, always—and he's been to see me two, three times since he's been out, that same prisoner. And them two licks.

Then you'd get a hold of one once in a while that's a 'gator. He's like from Missouri, he can take twenty-one licks and—well, for instance, when I first went to work up there they gave me a boy from Texas (they called him Texas), and I was loading sawdust and he sat down. I checked out and went out there to load the sawdust, and he sat down and told me he wasn't going to work. So I sent in for the warden, the warden come out there to talk to him, told him he'd have to work. He told him no, he wasn't going to work, so he carried him in there and gave him twenty-one licks. He was one of them kind, see; gave him twenty-one licks. So he brought him back, he got right back up there on that sawdust pile and sat down again, so I called the warden, told him he wouldn't work, so he come and got him, took him back in there and called Montgomery; they give him permission to give him twenty-one more, so they *give* him twenty-one more.

Well, he come back out there—naturally his tail had got in pretty bad shape, and his blood was showing up through his pants—so he just crawled right back up in that same place and he was going to show the rest of them prisoners that he could take as much of it as they could give. And, excuse the expression, this is what he said to the prisoners, he said, "I got more fanny than they got strap." That was the second time. He got up there and sat down and I sent back and got the warden, come back out there and tried to get him to go to work. He told him he wasn't going to go to work. So they carried him back in there and when they brought him back to me—I don't think they hit him but ten or twelve licks that last time—he told them he'd found out they had more strap than he had fanny, he could go to work. They brought him back and the blood had run down his pants to the bend of his knees and he got his shovel and went to work. Well, he worked about an hour, and I knew the boy wasn't in no shape to work, so I called them and told them that he was sick, he needed to go to the hospital. So they come and got him, carried him to the hospital, and put him in the hospital until his fanny sort of healed up a little bit. But that just shows you now if they had give in to that fella, he'd had undone everything that they had done up until then if they had let him got by. They *had* to conquer him, if they was going to run a prison. They had to get his attention. Yes, sir. Now, that boy happened out of my squad.

Now, I had another instance. I had a prisoner that was going free in the morning—his time was up the next morning—and he was from Texas (all them 'gators comes from Texas). So, I went out that morning and he sat down—we were digging stumps—he sat down on a stump and told me, says, "I don't intend to work." Well, I sent and got the man, there wasn't anything for him to do but to punish him. Didn't make no difference whether he was going free or not. If he hadn't punished him, then the other one before he went free he would have sat down so he couldn't work no more. That's what's wrong over there today. So, this boy sat down. So, he went in and they spanked him. Well, anybody that never had seen a prisoner spanked—after he's been spanked, a white man's buttocks turns blue, a nigger's buttocks turns white—and so he went to Atmore and got down there at Atmore. He just fell out over there in a ditch and somebody come out and picked him up; they carried him down to the doctor's office, right across from the drugstore. This fella come along and picked him up, and he asks him what was wrong, and he says, "I've been beat to death up there at the prison." So, they carried the man down there, took him in there to the doctor. Well, the doctor never had seen anybody spanked, so he dropped his pants and it was black, blue, so he got the man out on the street and everybody come down the street "come here, come here." So they called them in there and showed them this fella, see.

Well, they wrote it all up in the papers, advertisers and everywhere else and over—well, there wasn't no television then, radios and made a big bugaroo out of it. It never did amount to nothing, 'course it's just folks, just like I told you awhile ago, folks having sympathy for about as mean a fella as could be. They had a whole lot of talk in Atmore and wanted to run the warden off and all that sort of stuff, but it finally got straight, just like, well, somebody can rape a woman out here in this neighborhood and everybody in this neighborhood wants to kill him, right then. Six months from now, you take that same prisoner over here at the prison and him do something and you have to spank him, everybody in this country will be in sympathy with that fella over there. So that goes back to what Art Linkletter says, people are funny.

They done away with the strap and decided they would use some other method of discipline. So they got to burning up the cotton mill; every night they'd set the cotton mill afire. I was at Ketona at that time running a road camp, and they sent after me and the governor called out there and says, "We got to stop this mill being burned up, it's costing us too much money, we just can't afford to have it."

They hadn't mentioned anything about any other kind of discipline, so I went home and got me some hose pipe and carried it down in there in solitary confinement to where I could use it. I went to the dining room that evening—the shift that went to work at three o'clock was doing the burning up of the mill—so, I got up on the stage in the dining room and told them that I didn't want them burning up the mill to cost them anything: I was going to furnish the matches. All I wanted them to do was furnish the heads and whatever it took to go with it, that they wasn't going to burn that cotton mill up no more. So I says, "Now I'm going to punish every prisoner if he comes out of that mill until I get the right one tonight, if you set it afire." So, they went out and that mill hasn't been burned up no more since then. That wound up the mill.

They had little gangs there just like they got over here at At-more that was running over the other prisoners. I knew who was in the gang. I had a prisoner from north Alabama, a little ol' country boy, his folks was poor, and he come in the prison— I think he was in there for grand larceny, or some little ol' amount of something—so he come in my office crying and they had took his money away from him, three dollars, all his people had to send him. He hadn't had nothing to smoke, only what he begged, told me to get his money back. I asked him who got his money and he told me he couldn't tell me, he was afraid they'd kill him. And I told him, I says, "Well," I says, "If they bother you, I'll be responsible for it." So, he finally told me who it was and I sent and got them. Brought them up there and I asked him, I says, "Is them the boys that took your money?" And he said, "Yes, sir." So, I told them, I says, "I'll give you fifteen minutes to go get this boy's money and bring it back." And this one went out the office door and he turned back to him and said, "I'll get you." So they was back in about ten minutes, I reckon, laid the money down on the corner of the desk, and I asked the boy was that his money and he said, "Yes, sir," so I told him to take his money. I told them, I says, "Now instead of you all hurting this boy, I'm going to make you responsible for this boy. Whatever's done to this boy I'm going to do twice that much to you. If you break one of this boy's arms, I'm going to break both of yours, if you punch out one of his eyes, I'm going to punch out both of yours." I said, "Just dou-ble whatever you do to him, I'm going to do to you all."

So, I went up on the fifth floor, I called all the prisoners out and I had them all three standing side of me, and I told them the same thing I had told these three that took his money. Well, they never did bother the boy, and from then on I done away with the syndicate bunch, a gang bunch, that was in the prison. I done away with that.

The prisoners found out that I would help them, back them up, and anything that would come in the prison in just a few minutes I knew it was in there. They'd come tell me, says, "There's some dope in here, so-and-so's got it." "If so-and-so's got it tell me where it's at." Well, I'd go get it. Knives the same way, so when the knives got in there I knew about who had them. I'd take a box down there and put it in a cell, tell them, I'd say, "All right, I'm going to give you all a hour to put all these knives back in this box, all the knives you've got in this prison, and if I catch one on you now after I take the box up it's going to be me and you for it."

Well, I kept the knives and all that sort of stuff out of it: I didn't have a prisoner killed during the nine years I was there—and I don't think I had one cut. And the prisoners, they could lay their stuff down and the other prisoners wouldn't bother it.

It all boils down to this point: where you got discipline, you got control—that goes for homes, churches, towns, or whatever you want it to. If you hadn't got any discipline, you haven't got anything. In your home, you can go down the street and you can find a home where the children's running the home, you haven't got no home. That's the same way that's wrong with the prisons today, they haven't got no discipline, the prisoners is running it. And that's just what the lay of your troubles is right there.

If a man deliberately goes out there and beats a man up, he needs punishing for it, but if a prisoner violates the rules and you write up the rules for him to abide by, and he violates the rules, you hadn't punished the prisoner; the prisoner has punished himself! You see, in other words you wrote the rules up and give it to him; then if he violates it, he's the one that's done the punishing. The man that punishes man is not the one guilty man; the guilty man is the man that committed the crime. So there's where the federal government, I think, is missed the boat! 'Cause the judge, he runs his court, he sentences who he wants to, he gives them as much time as he wants to, he don't ask the prison system nothing about that. So naturally a man that runs a prison has got a job to do, too. I think you ought to make a report to the federal government what he does and put a report in the office at the capitol and all that sort of stuff, but far as controlling the prisoners, the man that is the head of that thing has got to control

it; if he can't control it, then he hasn't got any business there. If a
judge can't handle his court, then he hasn't got any business in
that court.

   When they did away with the strap, they burned them all, but
I had mine until somebody stole it. I had it in a sack and somebody
stole it—I don't know where it went. I had a special strap made
when I was at Ketona, and I run a prison at Ketona. And I punished my prisoners, put them right back on the same job they
was on. If they was trusties, I put them right back on as trusties;
I didn't write nothing up on the report, they went got a parole
when the time come; they went free when the time come. I never
did take nobody's good time. The prisoners liked that. In other
words, they liked for you to correct them and let it be between
you and them. And that's the way I handled it, just like it was a
family of my own. And I didn't have no trouble, just like I say, I
asked for two disciplinary reports during the nine years I was
there. I never did have to use the strap very much.

   At one time I had as many women as I had men at Ketona.
But you got to treat the women just like you do the men; they're
all men in the warden's sight. So I treated them all just alike. I
told my prisoners—my men prisoners—I told them, I says, "Now
these is my women, and if I catch you writing to one of them or
trying to talk to one of them, it's going to be me and you." I never
did have no trouble with them. Had them all in the same building;
had the women on one end and the men on the other.
   And they wasn't always black, no sir. There was as many white
give trouble according to the prison population as the colored.
The hard-headest man, the hardest man to control is a white man.
   Generally, I got along with the colored. I have never showed
any partiality in the colored or the whites. Or the women. I'd go
back as far as the women, when I had the women. They was all
prisoners and I had me some rules and regulations to go by. If
a prisoner broke them whether he'd be white or colored, he got
the same treatment. If a woman broke them, she got the same
treatment.
   Now, generally I had two or three young nigger girls, and I
had some young colored boys, that would do some little ol' friv-

olous thing—it wasn't much, but he needed a little punishment. I have really caught him up under my arm and spanked his fanny with my hand and put him down and that would straighten it out. So, I would never have to do nothing else to him.

And you can't have the same rules and regulations and you can't treat every prisoner alike 'cause there's no two humans alike, and you're dealing with human nature. So you've got to handle every problem with whatever it takes to handle it. There's no way to draw a line, say I'm going to do this, you're just as crazy as you can be. You can put you a road down yonder and you're first on this side then you're on that side, sometimes you're in the middle. You may come out at the same spot down yonder, but you can't go straight, you've got to give and you've got to take. The different problems.

Later the doghouse took the place of the strap, as I said, but I generally had a little extra on the side, I used too. But, right on the other hand, before I got Kilby straight, in other words, Kilby's in just about as bad a shape as Atmore is when I went there and they had done away with the strap. Well, naturally, I had to use every little thing I could use to hold up my discipline. Don't let my discipline go down 'cause if I did I knowed that I was gone. Well, they told me to use solitary confinement or the doghouse, but I went over on the river and got me some big white rocks, looked like about as big as a hen egg, poured me about an inch of concrete in it and laid them rocks in there where when he laid down in there he'd naturally have a lump under him. He couldn't be comfortable. Well, that got the job done until somebody told the governor what I had out there and he made me take that out.

But while I had that in—now to show how smart one of them is—while I had that in I give them a blanket and all to sleep on, wrap up in, and I had a little ol' boy in there that had a bar in there—had a prisoner that was bad to run away, and had to handcuff him at night and send a guard with him during the day, afraid he'd get away—I forget his name now, he was from Mobile County—but they had this cell fixed for him and they had a piece of bar up about waist high where he could stand up, with his hands handcuffed to the bar, or he could lay down; that bar

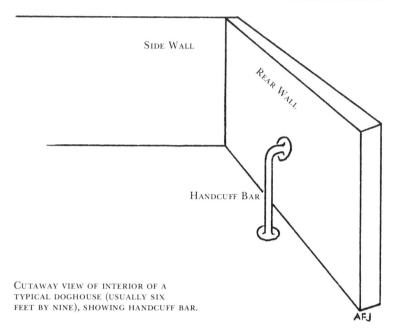

SIDE WALL

REAR WALL

HANDCUFF BAR

CUTAWAY VIEW OF INTERIOR OF A
TYPICAL DOGHOUSE (USUALLY SIX
FEET BY NINE), SHOWING HANDCUFF BAR.

AFJ

went clean to the floor, where he could lay down, and it come out
from the wall, set off about six inches from the wall. Well, I had
a prisoner that I put in there on this rough floor and he made
him a hammock out of the top of that thing and he was wadded
up in that hammock asleep! Sleeping as good there as I was sleeping at home! So I had to take his blanket away from him. That's
the reason I say you can't treat no two alike. Every situation is
different.

I carried a walking stick at Kilby all the time. A prisoner made
it for me out of hickory. I never did use it, only when a prisoner
acted like he wanted to not do what I wanted him to do—then
I'd hang it right around his neck. I hit him anywhere I could hit
him, anywhere there's anything sticking up. I didn't pick out no
certain place to hit him. If I took a notion to hit, I hit him.

I tell you what I done one night. We had prisoners that run
all the guards out of the cell at Kilby. And they called me to come
up there, and they was fighting in the cell. When I come in the
front door I went through the office and picked up a billet that

I had—Fred's got it now—a wooden billy club made out of hickory. And when I went in there, I told them to open the cell—there was about four-hundred prisoners in there—I told them to open the cell and they was all down in the back of the cell where they was fighting—where there was two men fighting—and ganged up around them, and one of the prisoners, this white prisoner, one of them turned around and seen me coming and he said, "Yonder comes Captain Dees and he'll hit the first man he gets reach of"—he hollered that out. And when I got to where the prisoners was fighting there wasn't but just them two there, they'd all done run up the stairways and got out of the way. I reached down there and got a hold of them and told, "You boys cut out that fighting," so they quit just like that, see. Well, they had done run the guards out of there and I went in there right by myself. 'Course that billet, they knew I would hit one of them.

One night I was right over here at Atmore—I was deputy warden and I was at Atmore and they called and told me they was out in the hall and they wouldn't go in their cells. So I went up there and they was out in front of the prison with shotguns and everything else and I drove up there and I said, "What's the matter?" They says, "The prisoners back yonder won't go in the cells." The guards had all done come up on the front, so I said, "Open them doors." They opened the doors, and I had me a good stick—well, I had the stick Fred's got, that's one I always carried for about fifteen, eighteen years. So they opened the last door and I went in there. I said, "You boys get in them cells." They just went to going in them cells just like that and I didn't have to hit a prisoner! Not a prisoner, but they knew I'd do it. That's the reason I said awhile ago, if they know you're going to do something, they're not going to do it, but if they know they're going to get by with it, then they'll do it. That's human nature.

Another time, after I went on the jail inspector's job and they had took me out of Kilby and made a man deputy warden that lived right next door to me, they called him and told him they had locked up the guards and some of the prisoners had went out the front—they didn't know how many—and took the guards' uniforms and wore them out. So he called me and asked me would I go up there with him and I told him I'd go up there with him.

I didn't know at the time the convicts took all the guards and
locked them in cold storage. And I got up there with him, he was
shaking like he had a chill and I told him, I says, "You ain't got
no business going in there in the shape you're in. You just stay
here and I'll go in there." So he stayed out on the front and I went
on in to Kilby and went on back through there; it was just as quiet
as—you couldn't hear nothing—felt like a ghost town. So I went
on back in the kitchen; I knew there's a bunch of prisoners in
there supposed to be fixing breakfast, see. We kept prisoners up
all night 'cause we run shifts in the cotton mill around the clock.
So I went on back in the kitchen. I couldn't hear or see a prisoner,
I couldn't hear one or nothing. Then directly I heard a door
rattle on the cold storage now, and I went there and took a meat
cleaver and knocked the lock off of it. There was six guards in
there with them billet clubs and all of the prisoners that worked
down there, all locked up in that cold storage. I turned all them
out, went on back up on the front, and the director, and others,
had come in on the front up there behind there and got down
there where the prisoners was out in the front. I walked up there,
says, "I got the guards out of the cold storage and turned all the
cooks out. I don't know how many of them are gone, I don't know
who's gone." Another says, "I just don't know how we'll find
out." I said, "Well, I'll find out for you."
    So I went. They had done put it on the radio that they was
out—didn't know who, but be on the watch out for a carload of
what looked like guards, but they was prisoners. And I went back
there to the first white cell block. The first cell on the right there
was a cook that worked out there on the front that cooked for
the guards, name was Curtis Howard. "Curtis," I said, "who is
it that's gone?" He said, "Aw, heck, ol' Sam Hamilton." And I
think he called three or four more. Says, "They took Mr. Williams
with a little ol' pistol awhile ago, and left out of here with him and
them guards." He named off them other prisoners, so I went
up there and told the director who all was gone. 'Bout that time
they caught them not far off and brought them back. Put them
on the dogwagon and put me behind them, sent me to Atmore
with them, locked them up. When I got back I had a letter telling
me it didn't make no difference if that thing was burning down,

for me not to go back in there. Then they made the remark that
I wasn't going to work back in no prison no more 'cause I retired,
and made a trade to be jail inspector. So I didn't go back. I ain't
been back in there since.

Kilby was the main prison. That was where the electric chair
was and that's where all the maximum-security men was and
that was the easiest prison in the state to run. I run road camps
and I run Atmore and helped run them all, but Kilby was the
best prison to handle your prisoners. They wasn't no way for
them to get out there hardly, and you could have different types
of things you could use to discipline them in there that would
offset the strap or whatever they would use.

I enjoyed working at Kilby the nine years I was there; they was
the easiest nine years that I ever worked to handle prisoners,
and I had around twelve- to fourteen-hundred prisoners all the
time. We had a huge, huge church and the hospitals, the TB
hospital and the regular hospital. Kilby was huge. We had the
cotton mill inside the wall, we had the tag plant inside the wall,
we could work all our prisoners in the cotton mill, and all the
medium-custody men, the men that didn't have too bad a record,
we could check them out on the farm; we raised all our stuff there
on the farm to eat. And so they done away with that prison and
bought this one down here and they've been having trouble with
it ever since.

Kilby had Death Row.* A man sentenced to the chair, he went
into Death Row. He stayed there until they commuted his sentence or electrocuted him. I went up there every day and talked
to them, asked them how they was getting along and all that sort
of stuff, which I went all over the whole prison every day. That's
something I don't reckon that any other deputy ever done. I

*Fred Dees, Sr.: "Death Row was a separate wing. And it was called
Little Alcatraz, mostly by the inmates, but the guards referred to it as
that too. The convicts gave it the name of Little Alcatraz 'cause Alcatraz, from what I can read and everything, had a reputation of being
pretty tough."

went all over the cell block, up on the fifth floor and all around and right by myself, inspected the prison, inspected the beds and go to the cotton mill, go through the cotton mill, tag plant—I made the round every day and visited the whole operation, went over the farm. In other words, I seen after the whole building. They had other men seeing after the jobs, but I'd go by and see if there was anything they needed me for.

They had the electric chair as far back as I can remember. And they electrocuted them, too—eight, nine, ten a year. When they went up there they was electrocuted. During the '50s and '60s it run anywhere from four to ten or twelve inmates on Death Row, I'd say. They kept them worked down pretty close. 'Course, you see when they give a man a death sentence he automatically gets an appeal. Automatically, it goes to the Alabama Supreme Court. Well, if they can find anything wrong in that trial, then they give him another trial. So whenever the Supreme Court rules on it and they don't find nothing wrong, everything is in order, then they electrocuted the man. Naturally that didn't build up a surplus.

Now, he also got a hearing before the governor. The day before he was to be electrocuted, like say he was going to be electrocuted tonight at midnight, which this is a Friday, they carried him to the governor today. We carried them down before the governor, their lawyer was there, the solicitor was there that sentenced them, their lawyer would make a plea for a life sentence and then the solicitor would get up and tell the governor about how the trial was and all that and what the man's guilty of and all that sort of stuff, and then the governor would decide whether to commute his sentence to life or let him be electrocuted. It was in the governor's office; right in front of the governor is where it happened, and the governor talked to him himself. Then they had all the court records there, too, you know. It took about, generally it took about a half a day. I'd say two hours or something like that, he was generally down at the governor's office. And sometimes the governor, he wouldn't give you a definite answer on that sort of thing until eleven o'clock at night. He'd call you and say, "Well, I'm going to let the law take its course." Or, "I'm going to commute that man's sentence to life in prison." Or, he could postpone it for a month. And sometimes you wouldn't know what he was going to do until maybe five minutes before you was getting ready to electrocute a man! Sometimes you'd done shaved his head and got him prepared to electrocute him and the governor would call, say, "Well, I've commuted this man's sentence to life in prison." So, then you turned him in to the population the next morning.

When they was electrocuting people, I would say for an electrocution offense there was about one in about five that got a life sentence. 'Course, I don't believe in leaving it; if twelve men gives a man the electric chair, and they heard the evidence, and give him the electric chair, then I don't think the governor ought to have the right over them twelve men to say that he'll give him life in prison. 'Cause it could be political with the governor. A governor could be satisfying a bunch of politicians, and them twelve men done said he was guilty, and they done sentenced him to the chair, I think that's enough, right there. If anybody commutes his sentence to life, it ought to be them twelve men.

Sometimes he'd stay on Death Row four, five years. He could appeal it, you know. Be sentenced to the chair and they'd take an appeal, and they'd take him back and try him maybe two, three times and maybe give him the chair every time they tried him, but he'd go back in there. Well you couldn't electrocute him until the Supreme Court reviewed the case and seen that everything was in order—all handled under the right form, like it ought to be. If there was any flaw in it at all, or any doubt at all in the conviction, the prisoner got the benefit of the doubt. Same way with my way of handling discipline; if I had any doubt of whether a prisoner was guilty or not, then I give the prisoner the benefit of the doubt.

They'd electrocute high as six, seven, eight maybe ten a year— it all depended on how many crimes was committed that carried the electric chair. Sometimes there wasn't but maybe one or two sent to the electric chair all over the state in a year. Well, naturally, there wouldn't be but one or two electrocuted in a year. It all depended on the men that committed the crimes that'd be electrocuted.

The date was set for them to be electrocuted and they electrocuted him one minute after midnight on Friday night. Now

for why I don't know, but they electrocuted every prisoner on
Friday morning right after midnight, on Friday morning they
electrocuted him. For what reason I don't know; that was the
procedure. It was done right at one minute after midnight.
I pulled the switch. Well, ah, the only way that I got assigned
to it was 'cause the warden had heart trouble. The law reads that
if the warden's sick, the deputy warden at that prison's got to do
it—at Kilby, that is where it was when I was there. The law read
that if the warden was sick then the deputy had to do it, then if
the deputy was sick then the director had to appoint a man, he
had to appoint a man to pull the switch. You couldn't just pick
up Tom, Dick, and Harry and go in there and kill a man.

I done it for four years. I worked under the warden; he had
trouble with his heart. I done it all for four years. 'Course he was
always standing there side of me, the warden was. Nobody knew
out in the audience whether he pulled the switch or I pulled the
switch. We was in a separate room. Was nobody in there but me
and him. There was a hole about four inches in diameter, and
they would have a little paddle there that said "ready" on one
side and "stop" on the other. So when they got the prisoner ready
to be electrocuted and everything and the doctor had done talked
to him, the preacher had done talked to him, and he'd done said
everything he had to say, then they'd put that little "ready" sign
up there, snap, you'd pull the switch. He never did know, he
never did know, he never did know what hit him.

He could order anything that he wanted to eat the night he
was going to get, the night he was going to be electrocuted, he
could order anything in the world that he wanted to eat, as much
of it as he wanted it was brought to him—steak, chicken, anything. Anything he wanted to eat, they give it to him.

The family could visit with him the day before. They could
stay in there and visit with him as long as they wanted to. The
families hardly ever, hardly ever came to witness. I don't remember ever seeing any prisoner's family there when that happened.
Now, they could claim the body and the state would ship it to
wherever it was sent up from, they'd ship it back to them. But,
generally—like a prisoner killed your wife, or killed your brother

or your father or something like that, and the man was sentenced
to the chair—generally them's the people that would come and
see that it was done.

They had, ah, they always brought a man into the electric chamber, fastened him into the chair, and ah, they asked him if he
had anything to say, did he realize what was fixing to happen
and he'd say, "Yeah," and you asked him if he had anything to
say, and the preacher would talk to him, pray with him or whatever he wanted to do. There was always a preacher there, a doctor
there, the warden there, the deputy warden was there, the elec-
trician, and the press, all that was there—and his family too, if
they wanted to be there! Or if he killed, like if he killed one of
your brothers and you wanted to witness the electrocution, they'd
let you in there, let you witness it too. But they had you fenced—
they had all the press and all the visitors fenced off away from
the chair. They could see the chair but they couldn't get to the
chair 'cause it was open, but they had a fence up there 'cause—
in other words it was dangerous, 'cause the chair sit on a rubber
mat, see, and a whole lot of times when a man is electrocuted his
water broke, see, and would run down and run on that mat and
run off and if you was to happen, if that water happen to get in
contact with you it would electrocute you too, see, while that
juice was on.

You pulled the switch, it was twenty-one hundred volts, or
twenty-one thousand volts, I believe, but anyhow it'd hit him all
at once and that'd kill him. He never did know what hit him.
Then it would cut itself off, then it would build itself back up to
twenty-one hundred volts again and it would cut itself back on
and then it would cut itself off. But during the time that you
pulled that switch and it built itself back up and cut itself off the
man didn't have no control over him; it was an automatic deal.
That gave him the juice twice. Then I've seen them, I've seen
them, ah, that wouldn't kill him and the doctor would examine
him and he would say, "This man is not dying, he's coming back
to." So the doctor then would order another shot, so then you'd
have to give him another shot, well that's the shot that generally
would, ah—there's a smoke, it would burn him little bit, burn

him where the leg-iron ground was and where it come in on top
of his head, it would burn him and cause a odor in that smoke,
you see, like you burnt flesh or something like that, and it'd get
in your clothes and you couldn't get it out.

Well, I got it, the first man I ever electrocuted, I got it in my
clothes, in that suit of clothes. (You always had to have on a suit
of clothes.) Well I sent it to the cleaners and they couldn't get it
out, so I just used it for that purpose from then on. But, ah, I
want to tell about the press and all that. I have seen them when
they'd electrocute a man, they'd just faint, just fall out just like
folks you'd shoot with a twenty-two rifle, just fall like that. Faint,
folks faint. You'd be surprised at the people that just can't stand
nothing hardly; they'd faint.

Then, you take right out here this morning, like I was saying
before, and, ah, somebody rape a woman over here, well everybody in this country wants a killing. When that happens, right
then they want a killing. Well, all right, you catch him and after
then send him to the electric chair, and go to electrocute him; or
he gets up there and kills some other prisoner or does something real bad and you have to correct him. These same folks
that wanted to kill him when he committed this crime will have
sympathy for him. So, you can't tell about human nature. People
are funny, people are funny.

You know, I've seen them walk in there, sit down in that electric
chair and never flinch—not a word. The warden would ask him,
say, "Well, you got anything to say," he'd say, "Not a thing, I'm
as guilty as I can be." Says, "I committed the crime, I'm guilty of
it, and I'm due the punishment."

Well, that's the same way they feel about discipline; that's the
reason I say you can't run a prison or nothing else without discipline. Any prisoner that's over there at the prison today knows
that you can't run that prison without discipline 'cause you got
to have discipline to take care of them that want to run over them
others that wants to do right. So they want a warden that's strict-
discipline man, and they want a warden that what he tells one of
them, he'll do. They want a warden that won't let them toughs,
that's we call them, run over the other prisoners. And that's what
this United States Supreme Court now is saying, you can't do

this, you can't do that. Well, I can't see how they going to run a prison without some kind, some kind of punishment that a man dreads; if you ain't got punishment that a man dreads or he respects, you haven't got no punishment.

The only two women that's ever been electrocuted during the time that I worked in the state—well, the only two women that's ever been electrocuted in the state of Alabama—was electrocuted at Kilby while I was deputy warden. One of them was electrocuted for killing her nieces and nephews, poisoning them and collecting the insurance on them; and the other was in there for killing her husband. 'Course, women, them two women was killed. A woman's head when you shave it is about as, about as, I don't know, in other words, a woman with her head shaved is about as ugly a thing as you ever looked at 'cause her head is not made like a man's. Did you know that? It's not shaped like a man's, it don't look like a man's; there's all the difference in the world in the shape of a woman's head and a man's head. And, ah, that electrocuting women bothered me worse than electrocuting men. 'Course, I looked at it from the standpoint—like that woman that killed all them children and collected that insurance, that she killed them kids, so she wasn't no better off, was no better than they was.

She was the first one. She just walked in there and sat down in that chair, just like she didn't pay it no more attention than nothing in the world—sat down in that chair and the doctor examined her and the warden asked her, says, "You realize what's fixing to happen?" She says, "Yeah." And the church preacher says, "You got anything to say now?" She says, "I just hope the people over there in Elmore County are satisfied." That's all that she said; she was just as sarcastic as she could be.

She was white—both of them were white. She was dressed in a prison uniform. Yeah, they had white dresses or blue dresses over there at the women's prison. She was in prison clothes. They brought her from Wetumpka over there, over to Kilby and put her in the Death Row for forty-eight hours before she was electrocuted. There was a matron stayed in there with her all the time. I think it was the deputy warden from Wetumpka that stayed in the room with her all the time she was over there, and

KILBY PRISON

they went on to the electric chair with her. Otherwise, there was just the preacher, press, stuff like that, was there. The warden signed the death certificate. The doctor made it out and the warden signed it. Well, the doctor had to sign it, too, you know.

I went to Kilby to go to work in 1951, I believe it was, 1950 or 1951, and I worked there until I come back to Atmore in 1961, I reckon somewhere along there. I was at Kilby about nine, ten years. I couldn't say whether it was the first year I was there—I know the first man that I electrocuted killed and raped; he killed a little baby and raped the little baby's mother at Calera, up there at Shelby County, and I know that. That's the first one I ever electrocuted, and I think that I got a piece in my purse that he put in the paper—he told the press that night how nice I'd been to the people that was in Death Row and he hoped that I'd continue to be thataway. I believe I've got a piece in my purse—I know I clipped it out—it was in my purse for a long time and I think I still got it.

I talked to the minister near 'bout every day. Not about the prisoners, but I talked to the minister, like I say he was in and out of the prison every day, and the doctors, too, I talked to all them folks every day.

Well, I'll tell you that thing is really worried me a whole lot 'cause the Bible says "Thou shall not kill." 'Course it goes on and says, in the Bible, some was killed during Christ's time. That, that "He put some to death," but the way I looked at it the twelve men that sentenced him to the chair was the twelve men that killed him. I just carried out my duties, I just fulfilled my duty. That thing has been on my mind more than anything, is that switch. But, on the other hand, somebody's got to do it. And when I took the job as deputy warden at Kilby I knew that that went along with it. I worked for the state twenty-one years 'fore I ever saw the electric chair! I never saw the electric chair until I went to Kilby as deputy warden.*

I got to come here tonight to a meeting. I'm on this water board. We got one of these government loans, you know, and put us in the water business; the government loaned us some money to put in a water system here and we buy the water from Atmore, and I'm vice-president and this man here in this house is president. He done called me last night and wanted to get us all down here for a meeting tonight. Evidently, we had a secretary that quit, and I imagine he's calling a meeting to appoint a secretary. I imagine that's what it'll be. We done got the water system in. I believe it's about one-hundred-forty miles of it, of the pipe. It goes up to McCullough; McCullough is about ten miles from Atmore. It goes to McCullough and it goes all around through this country here, and all around through the country between here and McCullough; then it goes out Highway 21 to that Interstate up yonder, goes out the highway we been on to the new prison, I mean to the prison farm—it goes out that highway to the Interstate up there. It's a big, big operation. About four hundred thousand dollars. We got the government to put it in.

---

*Fred Dees, Sr.: "That chair of his had a lot of bad on him. Oh, there's a lot of things about that chair. One of them called his name before he electrocuted him. That sure enough tore him up. Called his name out."

The jail inspector's job was part of the prison department. It must have been '55, somewhere around there, that I was jail inspector. You see, when a prisoner is sentenced to the prison, he automatically comes under the prison system, right then. So, they're supposed to have, the law requires them to have—they ain't got one now—but they're supposed to have a jail inspector go down and inspect these prisons and see if these jails are clean, see that these prisoners get plenty to eat and the beds are clean and all that sort of stuff. And security is in it, too. And they got, I don't know, I'm basically just doing a little guessing here, I think it's ten days after a man's sentenced that the prison department is supposed to pick that prisoner up out of the jail and brought to the penitentiary. I believe it's ten days.*

---

*From a United Press story dated August 30, 1975: "Montgomery, Ala., Two federal court judges ordered Alabama yesterday to stop accepting any new inmates until the populations at four state prisons drop to the levels for which they were designed.

"U.S. District Judges Frank M. Johnson Jr. of Montgomery and William Brevard Hand of Mobile said the state prisons could accept only apprehended escapers and former prisoners who have had parole revoked.

"The two judges said 'the serious overcrowding' and serious lack of custodial officers' results in the almost complete inability on the part of the Alabama prison officials to control violence within these prisons.

" 'This violence includes, but is not limited to, stabbings and sexual assaults by inmates upon other inmates, on a regular and continued basis.'

"To deny emergency relief, Johnson and Hand said, would continue to subject the inmates to 'these serious constitutional deprivations.' The judges ruled on a suit filed on behalf of inmates of the state prison system."

From the Atmore *Advance,* September 4, 1975: "Associate Prison Commissioner Walter Capps, who is serving as acting warden of Holman Prison and Fountain Correctional Center, said that it will probably be a long time before the Atmore prison population is reduced to proper levels.

The prison system made all the prisoner' clothes, made all
their underwear, all the sheets, all the pillow cases, all the mattresses, all the blankets. Made everything they used in the city
jails. I took their orders for their clothes and everything. That
was in cities with ten thousand people in them or less. The jails
used to use—when he get in jail they'd put prison clothes on him,
white clothes, with a number on it—then they used prison-made
sheets, prison-made mattresses, prison-made socks, all prison-
made underwear. And we'd send it to them. Also, we sold them
canned goods that we canned at the canning plants, but now they
haven't even got no canning plant, I don't guess. So, I'd sell
them all that sort of stuff. And the insane asylum, we'd sell them
theirs. And the University of Alabama, we sold them a bunch of
sheets and stuff, blankets and all that sort of stuff. But whenever
you go to selling the universities, the state universities now I'm
talking about (the private universities wouldn't buy it, but the
state universities would buy it), you got to come in to competition
with the outside labor and it's got to be right up to snug or they
won't buy it. But we was making good enough that they was buying it.

That was the jail inspector's job. Afterwards I went back to
being deputy warden at Atmore.

Now I know discipline is one of the things that prisoners com-
plain about today, but it goes back to this: everything you do today they run and say you violated his civil rights. In other words,
I can tell you, you're walking down the road out there, and I tell
you, I say, "I don't want you to walk on my side of the road, I want
you to walk on that other side." You say, "Well, you violating my
civil rights, I can walk on any side I want to." So, they've got too

"Fountain, which was built for 632 inmates, held 1,133 prisoners
Wednesday morning. Holman, a 550-inmate maximum security prison,
houses 848 prisoners.

"In the federal court order, the state was not given any time limit
in which to get the prison population down to acceptable levels, Commissioner Capps added."

much of this here stuff, that sort of stuff in there and in the running of the government. Everybody claims he's got his rights for
this and rights for that; there's nobody who can control nobody.
It's civil-rights laws that actually caused the change.
    Unless you really mistreat somebody, I don't think you've
violated their civil rights. If you deliberately meet a colored man
in the road and beat him all up, you've violated his civil rights;
but if you've got a home here and he comes out here and wants
to come in and sit down in your home and do as he pleases and
you tell him he can't do it, this is your home, I don't think you've
violated his civil rights. 'Cause if you can't protect your own home,
then who's going to protect it?
    Civil rights. They started integrating prisoners whenever
they passed the law.* If they had to integrate them, that's when
we started to integrate them. We had whites in some cells and
colored in the others. We had, they run about 60 percent black
and the rest of, 40 percent white. And, honestly, honestly, I think,
I really believe that the prisoners had to take a choice, the colored
and the white, to have separate cells today, I believe if you was
to give them that choice, they'd do it. I don't think they want to
mix. That's just like a quail—trying to make a quail go with a
dove or one of these little ol' town sparrows go with a pigeon. In
other words, if we'd all been made to be the same, the Lord would
have made us all the same. So I believe in the Bible myself; I think
He fixed us this away and He intended for us to be separated.
If He hadn't done it, He would have made us all just alike. You
don't see no blackbirds mixing with no quail.
    Now, this is a private school. Private school, folks from Atmore
and everywhere sends their kids here. They don't send their
kids to a regular school, just send them to a private school. That's
the cafeteria there. That's a private school for this country. They
got one in about every town in this country 'cause they don't want
to mix them up. That's the reason I said you can go down to one
of these schools, we can drive to one of them schools in Atmore,

---

*A three-judge federal court in Montgomery ruled on December 12,
1966, that Alabama's compulsory segregation in jails and prisons was
unconstitutional and had to be eliminated on all levels within one year.

public schools, you'll see all the colored together, you'll see all the whites together. So that's the reason I say they don't especially want to. You'll run into some smart class of them that wants to push they self on white people, but they're different!

You can take one of them and put him under a shower and turn the shower on him and run it all night, let the water run on him all night, and it won't wet him! Did you know that? That's right. You pull him out from underneath there he's just as dry as a chip, the water runs off of him just like he's greased. We cut the hair off—they kept the hair cut off so we could wash his head. You can let the hair get on him that long on his head and it won't never get wet. It's like wool; it turns water, it won't get wet, and it'll get your linen just as dirty as it can be 'cause he puts grease and stuff on his hair trying to get it straight, see, and he just keeps your linen, your sheets and your stuff like that, keeps it so nasty until the inspector will come in and he'll want to know what in the world's the matter. Well, 90 percent of the people all over the country don't know that you can't wet a nigger. You wet him! I've been in bathing with them; he come out, dive in the creek, come out, shake himself and there wouldn't be a drop of water on him! He don't have to dry off. He's automatically dry. You can run water on him all night and you can't wet his head! And he's got a scent that a white man ain't got, too.

After integration the colored naturally felt like they was getting a break, you know, somebody was leaning a little to them over the whites, and naturally a certain class of colored would try to run over some weak white prisoner, or something like that. That was about the only trouble we had with it, was something like that. But any prisoner that had any good common sense and all, he knowed that the law said you had to do it, just like the army. They know when they go in the army that's what's going to happen to them. They accepted it. They all eat out of the same pot. They all eat in the same dining room. The white used eat on one side and the colored eat on the other, and I think today that, if you leave it up to them to make their choice, they'd all want it done the same way. The only thing, the only change it made, it let them move over there to eat together. Whites and colored mixed up together to eat. Before, they could sit wherever they wanted to. They all got to take food at the same table, they all got their plates out of the same box, but where they come around at the table, like that, and come off like this, the colored would be on this side and the white on this side. The white would go back and sit down on one side of the dining room and eat, the colored would sit on the other side of the dining and eat. And all the food come out of the same pot. Afterwards, they made them all go in the same line. If a colored come up, or two colored come up, and got where he was going ahead of one white, then they all went on, the two colored went on ahead of the white. In the row. When they got to the table the guard was filling up the tables as they come to them.

Now, there's all this talk about rehabilitation. Well, I had a prisoner one time that was a bully at Kilby. This boy was from Texas—a great big Texas boy. He told them, "I'll tell you now, I ain't scared of that fella Dees, he ain't gonna bother me." He just beat up on them boys back there awful. Well, I had to wait until he really done something that I could say, "You done this." So, he whupped a little ol' boy one evening and that little ol' prisoner come up there and told me about it, so I went back there and got him. I got his attention and put him in the doghouse. The next morning I went down there and seen him. He says, "Captain Dees, you know if my daddy had a done what you done to me last night, if my daddy had a done that to me, I wouldn't have never been in the penitentiary. I'd never come to the penitentiary."

And 90 percent of the people in the penitentiary, their mothers and fathers are the cause of it 'cause they didn't make them behave their self at home. And they wouldn't make them work. Now, they can talk about all the rehabilitation programs they want to, and all that stuff, [but] if they'll just do three things, they've done a good thing for a prisoner. If he can't write, learn him how to write—read and write. I think everybody ought to know how to read and write. And learn him how to work, that's the main thing; there's 95 percent of them don't know how to work—they never have worked none. Then learn him discipline. If they'll learn a prisoner them three things, which won't cost the state one nickel, they have done one of the best jobs that ever has been done in a prison. Now that's the way *I* see it.

And this Texas boy had a college degree. That's another thing that I say that rehabilitation is not the answer, learning them a trade is not the answer. It might be on one or two, but I go back to the three things that I just said—work and read and write and learning discipline. They've got men up there that's the finest bookkeepers, they've got men up there the finest drawing artists, they've got men up there that are the best mechanics, the best welders, carpenters, and anything else that you want—they got them. And the time that they get out, they get right back in, so learning them a trade is not the answer. Learning them a trade is not the answer, so I say they're just spending a bunch of money that they could keep for other purposes instead of throwing it away like that.

We had around two guards at night, not over three men when we had seventeen hundred prisoners in the prison back in 1934 and on up to 1950, you might say, or '55 or maybe '60; then they begin to put in all these new programs and all that sort of stuff. Then they got you hiring psychologists and all that sort of stuff and begin to hire—in other words, they quit hiring common men with common sense. It got to where you had to have a twelfth-grade education and you had to have a degree in college to be a deputy warden. I'm not knocking education, now; a man that's— our smart men that's got a college degree is generally our bankers, our preachers, and all our smart people that's running these, head of big corporations and things like that. But now the biggest fool that I ever saw is an educated man that ain't got no common sense. You can't tell that fella nothing and you can't show him nothing and he is undoubtedly just like a wild cow—you can't head him; the way you head him he's just like a goat, that's the way he goes. You can't tell him nothing, you can't reason with him, you can't do nothing with him. So he just hasn't got any common sense whatsoever, and you just got a man there that's just in a rut, and I think he's in worse shape than a man that don't know how to read and write! I think that when you get a man that's got a degree, in psychology more than anything else, to begin with he puts himself so much above a convict, your convict, by him doing that, he resents it.

Anyhow, just one prisoner out of a thousand that's got a criminal record, that's been a criminal for ten or fifteen or twenty years, then he gets out on a parole, makes a complete change. He'd been out on parole before then; he didn't do right good. So that's just one out of a thousand. Now there's a world of prisoners—not a world of them, but there's a whole lot of prisoners gets in one time and they don't never get in any more. Them kind of prisoners is out on parole and things like that and they'll stay out. But you take a man that's been in three and four and five times on different charges and he's not going to stay out. Just one out of a thousand that'll stay out. 'Course not many now that's got a criminal record will stay out. If he's got a criminal record of just going out and coming back, going out and coming back, well he won't stay out, he'll come back. Don't make no difference how much supervision you got. It's not going to happen, no.

That's the reason I suggested even if a man was born thataway, born—he's either going to be a preacher, he's going to be a doctor, he's going to be—in other words, I think all our smart men got college degrees and got good common sense is in all our schools, all our banks and our factories and all that sort of stuff. In other words, just like a doctor, if he's cut out to be a doctor he'll be a doctor, if he's cut out to be a banker he'll be a banker, if he's cut out to be a law-enforcement man he'll be a law-enforcement man. I don't think a law-enforcement man will make a good prison man, though. Like one out of a thousand of them will make a good prison man. One's to catch a man and convict him and the other's to take care of him and keep him straight while he's in the penitentiary. So there's no comparison to the jobs at all.

We had at that time—that was during the Depression—that you could hire good, settled farm men. In other words, you could hire men with good common sense that you could sit down and explain something to and they'd understand it. And they made you your best prison guards. I think a sheriff or a policeman or an army officer, or anything like that, be just as much out of place as I'd be in the pulpit trying to preach. They hired men according to the duty he could do; they didn't go by his education.

A good man with good common sense is all you need over there, 'less you want him to keep books or something like that.

Then it got down to coloring them out and that made it harder to get your personnel, and then you'd get personnel you didn't want—this, that, and the other. Another example. They got them a band now—they're going all over the country playing the band. Well we had that, too, until they finally rape somebody or run away, about half of them, and tie the guard up and left him or something like that. They got a bunch going out now talking to these city organizations, civic clubs, and all kinds of city organizations. That's another one of them hats, now, they're toting around. And they've got it on the warden and naturally they going to put it on somebody else, I read a piece in the paper this week where they was up at Flomaton, made a talk to the Chamber of Commerce up there, and a preacher got up, a free man—generally, they'll put it on a preacher quicker than anything else—but this preacher got up and told the people, he says now that shows you that the people don't know what's going on in the prisons, that these prisoners want to *help* people, they want to help people, keep them from getting in prison, keep people out of prison and all that sort of stuff. Well, they got that hat right down there around his neck! He can't breathe, you see! They've really got that hat on him! *That's* rehabilitation.

They always want to blame the prisoner; it's the free people and the system they got is what brings all this thing down, and it all boils down to one thing—discipline.

What's my idea of the best penal system? Well, I think you need to have—I would be for rehabilitation to this point: if a man couldn't read and write, learn him how to read and write, and learn him how to work, and learn him discipline. If the state of Alabama would learn every prisoner that they have to come in the penitentiary; if he couldn't read and write—I think that's the main thing—to learn him to read and write and to learn him discipline is three things that—the reason he's in the penitentiary is 'cause he hasn't had no discipline at home, and another thing is 'cause he won't work.

Did you know that 90 percent of the young today won't work!

Did you know that? They won't work. When this crowd you all's
age is gone, what these young folks going to do? They're going
to starve to death. You ever think about that? They just won't
work. Few of them will, but there ain't enough of them to work
to feed the rest of them!

This was prison farm, all farm out here. There's nothing here
like it used to be. There was a little over four hundred miles of
terrace. That's a terrace, see that there? There was over four
hundred miles of that on this property at one time, when we had
mules here. See all that land over yonder? We worked every bit
of that; now they're not working none of it. They're working
right up and down south of the road here. See over yonder where
they're not working? We worked all that land. Corn and stuff—
we fed the prisoners with it. We had our own grist mill; we made
our own meal. Raised our own rice in these low places—had
our rice mill. We made lye hominy out of corn. You take corn
and shell it and then you take it to the canning plant and you run
it through a lye water—wash it in lye water. That takes all that
hard substance off of it and just leaves the kernal in there. Then
that's what's washed and rewashed and washed again and canned.
That's where you get hominy. Now, the lye part of it is referred
to as the lye that you put on it to get the hard substance off of it
down to the hominy. But if you'd go into a grocery store to buy
it, you'd ask for hominy.
    Well, we used everything we raised, we used. Even in the road
camps and all. We had a canning plant here; everything we
couldn't eat, we canned it. We didn't waste nothing; we canned
it, so there was nothing went to waste.
    I've seen acres and acres of peas up here last year, regular peas
that you canned. They planted for a cannery and let the worms
eat them up, let them get full of worms and all and they wasn't
fit to can—they wasn't fit to eat at all. Just acres and acres of them
and they couldn't pick them, they didn't have no—they couldn't
make these prisoners pick them.
    There's a bunch of prisoners there. That truck, they're going
to do something down the other way, they went the other way.
But you used to, could see here a mile, right down this swamp

here; we had it cut out, every bit of it cut out. It was clean. Everywhere you could clean out to where you could see. That's security, that helps your security. So we tried to keep everything cleaned out so we could see. 'Course, now they don't do it anymore. They don't put them down there in that swamp 'cause they're afraid they'll run away—and they will, now. But I kept my dogs down there with me, and if a man run away I caught him there quick. Well, the dogs aren't as good as they used to be, nohow. The dogs is all down yonder in the pens; they don't do that no more.

Now there's a squad on their way to work. That's really a good guard there on that horse. Now that's just—the few prisoners they're checking out, out of two thousand prisoners! And that one over yonder, Holman, that one over yonder don't check out nobody. They can't work this farm without—it takes about seven hundred, eight hundred men to work this farm. There ain't more than forty or fifty, I think there's about a hundred altogether they checked out. And the rest of them's in there playing ball and all that, studying up some kind of damned meanness to get into. You see they ain't going to work this, don't look like they're going to do a thing here. 'Course, over yonder, right side of the road, they make the people think they're really putting on the dog, see, right alongside of the road.

Now all that equipment out yonder you see is not the state of Alabama's; they rent that equipment. It used to all belonged to us, but they claim they can rent it cheaper—save money. But don't you know that common sense will teach you now that if a company can rent them equipment and make money off them, the state can really buy their own equipment and save money? Common sense will teach you that. So they hadn't got no argument at all to base their opinion on.

I'm going to carry you up here and show you a ditch that's twenty-six, I believe it's twenty-six feet deep. We threw all the dirt up on a scaffold and then throw it on out, and I helped dig that ditch. There. It was used to drain a big pond. Now, we used to have rice in all them ponds in there. We raised our rice. People don't drive out here where me and you are at, to see what's going on, 'cause if they did they'd raise more hell than a little. But me and Fred has really killed a many a bird on this place.

Now that's the pond we was draining, that big pond over yonder where them trees are. They let it grow up. Its water stands in there the year around. See how they've let it cave in? And that ditch when it's cleaned out, it's twenty-six feet deep. They let it cave in. They could take two guards and bring a hundred men over and put in that ditch, and one stand at this end and one stand up yonder at the other end, ain't no way for them to get out; two men could work a hundred men in there. Well they don't use no common sense on what they're trying to do. I could work every prisoner they got up there three hundred and sixty-five days a year for the next twenty-five years and never catch up. They can't drain the lake, the ditch done filled up. That's what I'm talking about—all them men up yonder in that yard, they could bring them over here and work them, right there in the ditch. And a tired man ain't going to give you no trouble.

And the state of Alabama has got to feed them; they can't run off. It ain't like a factory or something like that: "We don't need you, you all go home." You can't send these things home; you got to keep them. So it don't cost a bit more to keep him and work him; if he just digs a hole and turns around and fills it back up, you still give him something to do, the prisoner. His health's better, he better off in every way to take exercise; you're not only getting the prisoner tired to where he'll rest, but he won't give you no trouble. You're also helping the man to stay physically in shape to do anything he wanted to do, if he was to get out.

It's not punishment. Well, if it is then they're punishing every man that's working in these factories and things trying to make a living and paying taxes to feed these things. Them's the men that they're putting the punishment on, the working man. If they going to sit the prisoner down and fan him and feed him for getting out here and holding up a bank or raping somebody, then the man that's having to pay the taxes, he ought to say they're discriminating, they're violating my civil rights. 'Cause he's got a perfect right to say that, 'cause he's working to feed him and the prisoner's not doing anything. And he can't stay in society, he won't behave himself.

Now, they could send a bunch of men right there and fix some shells where the road's washed out here. You could get that to where you got to drive over it. Instead of it they're driving around it over the farm, down in the field. Them's the things that need it now. I didn't have none—I just wouldn't put up with that sort of work at all. It had to be right or I'd be running somebody off. 'Course, I wouldn't have the job and worry with it; as old as I am, I couldn't. My health wouldn't stand it.

Now, this state property starts again, right here, see. They're planting something right down yonder. That's a prison crew down yonder, these's free people's land over on this side. I may know this guard. Yeah, that's ol' Hopkins.

"What's you say here, Mr. Dees?"

"Hello there, Farmer Hopkins, how you getting along?"

"Pretty good."

"Boy, I didn't know that you took a course in agriculture?"

"You didn't! Yes, sir."

"This fella, he's from California and he wanted to see our prison system and that sort of stuff, and he's taking some pictures of the farm and all. . . ."

"He can look at anything he want to look at, but I don't know nothing."

Under the system they got now nobody knows what's going on but the heads of the thing. The time that I worked for them, or started work for them—it got to the last where we didn't know nothing either—but whenever I started to work with the prison system everybody knew what was going on in the prison system 'cause we didn't have, just like I say, we didn't have but four-hundred thousand dollars to operate on. And we had about seven thousand prisoners in the state. We rented our biggest portion of them to the Highway Department; they paid us so much per month for them, and we used that to help take care of the other prisoners at the camp.

Now they've done away with that. And they spent twenty-one million dollars last year, and they've got crops that they've plowed under that they couldn't even get. They can't even get them together! They can't even make them prisoners work!

And it's a bad situation when you can't make a prisoner work and the taxpayers in the state of Alabama has to feed him just like he's a millionaire and let him look at television and all that sort of stuff, when he won't stay in public, they can't leave him on the public because he won't behave himself. So I'm just against it. I believe they ought to have to work and try to make enough to feed theyselves, anyhow. I think the change in the personnel of the higher officials in the last twenty years has had more to do with it than anything else. I don't think you can put the blame on the little man when the little man hasn't had any backing, he hasn't had any cooperation. If a prisoner cussed him out, he'd go to the warden, the warden wouldn't do nothing with the prisoner and the prisoner would go back by the guard and laugh at him or cuss him again, so he wouldn't carry him back up there 'cause he just turned him loose for cussing him out. So I blame every bit on the high officials, every bit of it. And it goes back to what the ol' red nigger said, "If a man don't know, he just don't know."

I don't think they know what they're trying to do. It still goes back to the officials for not backing the guard up. The officials got scared, they got scared, and they want to take the responsibility, well if he's got a job or head of the department, the board of directors, then they ought to take a stand against the federal government that they got to control these men, and they got a job to do just like the judges has got a job to do or the sheriff has got a job to do; they got a job to do to take care of them and make them behave themselves and to protect the other prisoners. So they wouldn't take a stand against the federal government, then naturally the little man he can't do nothing, no more than he's backed up to do. It still goes back to the officials. It's easy for the officials to say, "I can't do so and so 'cause the federal government won't let me do it." He needs to put up an argument with the federal government and show the federal government where he's got to control these prisoners.

Any warden, he's scared to death, but the director in Montgomery will tell the warden, say, "Don't do so and so." It all goes back to the director, the higher men. The higher men ought to take a stand against the federal government and tell the federal judges that they have got to—if they won't have nothing to do with what they give a man to serve in a penitentiary, they don't have nothing to do with that—so long as they don't just deliberately beat a man to death or get out and beat a man up for nothing, then just in line of duty they have got to have leverage over them to make them behave themselves. They can't just turn them loose. And that's what they've done.

There ain't no prisoner ever been beat to death. I stayed with them thirty-eight years and I never did know of a prisoner getting beat to death, and I never did know of one getting hit that didn't need it, 'less they hit at him and happen to miss him. That would be my experience of what I done; [unjustified punishment] might have gone on, but where I was at the prisoners that got punished, they needed punishing. And without it, it would be in the same shape it is today. The prisoners couldn't exist in there without getting killed. The record's over there to show for itself: they killed about seventeen over there last year, and I bet you they killed eight or ten already this year.* Inmates and guards, too. They killed two guards this year. One at Holman and one at Atmore.

The ones that want to run over the other prisoners, take what he's got and don't want him to say nothing about it, and they don't want you to do nothing about it, and if you do something, then they'll holler, "You've violated my civil rights." It just gives one side, it gives the side where you corrected it; it don't give the side that he just went down there and took money away from a prisoner and that's the reason that you done it. But it's a one-sided deal.

Say, that bunch there in Mobile—I've been reading something in the paper—they just been putting one side of things in the paper and that's what a prisoner writes and tells them. And a prisoner's going to tell it like he wants it to sound, see. He's not going to tell no side that would look bad on him, he's going to tell the side that looks good for him. The one that does that sort of stuff is the small, it's a small minority of them, but they're there anyhow and they got to be controlled. And they haven't been controlled. I don't know what they're going to do with them.

---

*January through March, 1974.

I would recommend putting back the strap for the prisoners that no other discipline will take care of. And then I'd recommend the solitary for prisoners that wasn't so hard to get under control. And then there's a certain class of prisoners that you can sit down and talk to and get them to do right. But there's a certain class of prisoners in the prison system, federal or any other prison system, that's from Missouri; you got to sight them folks that you mean business, that you mean for them to behave themselves, and you got to have punishment that they dread or they won't pay no attention to you.

I don't believe in punishing a man until he does something, and be sure you're right when you do have to punish him. But when you tell them, say, "Now don't you do this; if you do, I'm going to put that strap on you," if he does it, put that strap on him.

Of course, I'm still for the strap, and I think the time is fast coming back now where you're going to see the courts, the courts get tighter. The courts got loose on criminals first, see, the Supreme Court especially. Then the criminal courts, they got light on them, and the penitentiaries got light on them. Then they begin to get this civil rights all mixed up with it. Well, a man's got forty years in there for rape or murder, to my way of seeing it he's done forfeited all his civil rights, he hasn't got any civil rights and so I think the time's coming, and it's coming mighty fast, where you're going to see stricter discipline through your country than you have in the past. 'Cause they're going to have to have it. The Bible says it—it's as plain—it says you got to have discipline. It plainly says, "Use the rod."

So, they intend for you to get a man straight, get them straight if they get wrong. They talk about murdering people and all that sort of stuff. Well, they do in these other countries, and if our country was more strict about it—they talked about one time putting in this habitual-criminal law that a man comes to the penitentiary three times, then the fourth time he comes there he wouldn't get out no more, see. Well, I told them, says, "You're not doing a thing in the world—a prisoner probably wouldn't give you no trouble if you'd just leave him hanging where he didn't know if he was going to get a parole or not. But if you tell him he's going to stay there the rest of his life, well he hasn't got anything to live for, he'd just as soon kill you or anything to get out." I said, "You're just asking for it," and I says what I would do. I says, "Now a whole lot of folks would criticize me for saying a thing like this, but before I put in a habitual-criminal law, to put him in there for life, I'd say, 'All right, when he comes back here four times for a felony we'll just electrocute you—get you out of the way.' "

So that's the thing to do, is get the man out of the way. Every time he gets more time and all, he's subject to more to stay outside; there's no telling how many he'd kill to get to stay outside. Well the best thing to do when you get a man in that condition is to go ahead and get him out of the way. So if we had a law like that in Alabama, you wouldn't see all these penitentiaries full of prisoners and all that sort of stuff. I didn't have a prisoner cuss a guard, much less hit him! I just wouldn't put up with it.

Now then, take him up there to court and he cusses the judges out and makes a plumb scene in the court and they got him up there and they get some lawyer that's with the NAACP to represent him, so they'll drag it out in court and he'll get up there and pop off. I was in court the other day, one of the jurors; they wouldn't put me on none of the cases 'cause they knew how I felt about it. They brought a boy in there for, I think he stuck a guard with a knife, and he come walking in and you could tell he figured he was bad. So they sat him down there and he sat with about a half grin on his face like he's done something real pretty. I got out of there about as quick as I could get out. When they dismissed me off the jury, after this panel of jury at the crime, they let the rest of us go home, so I got out of there. They wouldn't put me on no jury. They'd knock me off of every one of them. Right quick. And anybody that was sitting around where I was at—they didn't put them on there neither. There was a lawyer there from New York representing this boy, so the solicitor told them . . . him, says, "Dees is a retired man from out there," and says, "he knows the prisoners and he knows the guards too," says "I'd love to have him on this jury." (That was before they started striking the jury and we wasn't in there then; I heard about it later, see.) And this fella from New York says, "Noooo, I'm not going to have him and I'm not going to have none of them

fellas that sits around where he's at either. He'll influence them
to vote just like he wants them to."

   And the prisoners are supposed to be in a uniform, where you
can tell a prisoner from a free man. Over yonder at our prison
the guards has got on a uniform and the prisoners has got on
street clothes! So you can't tell who a prisoner is, but you can tell
who a guard is 'cause a guard's got on a uniform. They just got
it visa versa!*

   Last year, last year alone, a state senator told me that they give
the prison system around twenty-two million dollars—and they
spent it. Now they're asking the legislature to give them forty
million dollars! So they won't have to work. The taxpayers—
they ought to rebel against that outfit and run them out of the
state of Alabama. There's an outfit in California trying to come
over here now and buy blood from them, like they used to have.
Buy blood from them, blood plasma, and they'll pay so much.
Well, they hadn't put that in; they put it in one time when I was
with them, and they got so crooked with it and something happened to them. I don't know just exactly what did happen, but
it wasn't above the board and they made them do away with it. So
they hadn't put it in yet, but they're still talking about it. Reason,
I read it in the paper.

   The prison department's got a board over it, Board of Corrections, and they did have, they started off with three and I think
it was, then they increased it to five. God help them knows how
many they got now. They used to have one warden and one deputy warden. Over here alone they got two or three wardens and
five or six deputy wardens. And we had one captain, one lieu-

---

*Fred Dees, Sr.: "I went over there to see a convict about buying some
purses and billfolds to put in the shop that my daughter Faye had?
Daddy and I was sitting there and he said, 'Son, I want you to notice
what's happening.' And in just a few minutes the guards would come
in, and—I actually seen this now, this ain't no hearsay—they shook the
guards down and the convicts walked in and out of the front gate without even them putting a hand on them. But the guards, now, they shook
the guards down. I seen that!"

tenant, and a sergeant. I expect you can't stand the sergeants and lieutenants out there in that yard! They'll get a man and he's on probation for six months; well you got six months to get rid of him. Well, he'll get in there and probably have a little politics behind him and all; first news you know the six months has run by and they can't get rid of him then unless they fire him, so they just put him over in the corner somewhere on some kind of job. They can't cut his wages 'less he does something, so they just put him over to the side and make him another deputy warden. Then they got two, and if that don't prove out, they'll put him over on the side and appoint them another. So first news you know they got five or six deputy wardens there. Old saying is, "They got more chiefs than they got Indians."

The criminals has absolutely took this country over. A criminal is treated better than a man that's a law-abiding citizen! He's got more rights, he's got everything, everything's in his favor. A criminal. I hate to say that, but that's exactly the sort of shape our country's in. 'Cause our country's supposed to be a Christian country, but it's turned out to where it's everything but a Christian country. Now, I don't know just what's going to happen, but it ain't going to run long like it's running. I believe the Good Master's going to pull the plug out of it. I sure do.

The first thing you got to do, the first thing the prison system's got to do is put a man in Montgomery that'll run the prison system, put them some rules and regulations in there. The courts has got to get off of it and let it alone. The prison system don't fool with the courts' business so the courts has got to let the prison alone. They can send them to the prison, but they got to let the prison system run it. The courts has got to let it alone. That's the first thing's got to happen. Then you got to get some folks over here that'll back the guards up and put them prisoners back in some prison clothes, put them prisoners back in them prisons, and put them back to work and stop all this here "who shot John" stuff they're doing and start to making some grub for their own use instead of the taxpayers having to feed and fan them. That's what they're doing now. Buying them televisions to look at and sitting there and got a free man fanning them. That's just about a good illustration of it right now, the way it is. And not only in this state, in other states, too, the whole criminal system in the whole United States is broke down. The FBI says the same thing. J. Edgar Hoover said the same thing before he died.

They don't need no more prisons; they don't need no more money. They need to run and do just what I'm saying. They need to go back there like it was whenever after the World War, we didn't have nothing to eat, we had to work to make something to eat. Well, them folks over there ought to have to work to make them something to eat.

Now you can't have every county with it's own prison, either. It would cost the counties, it would cost the counties so much that I don't believe that the counties could afford it; I believe it would break them. The big counties like Jefferson and Mobile—the counties that's got the big cities in it—they could figure out some work program. But you take Escambia, Monroe, and Conecuh, counties like that, that would have a hard criminal to get in the penitentiary, they wouldn't have nowhere to keep him and they couldn't work him and they couldn't do anything with him. So, they're going to near about have to have a penal system of some kind.

I'll tell you something else. The thing is so complicated now, you're guarding over there and it's your day off, one of your days off—you get two days a week off—and if it happens to happen on one of your days that you got a prisoner wrote up for some sort of charge and they going to try him on one of them days and you live in Mobile, you got to come back up here that day of the trial! They don't believe one thing that you say, so if you're not going to back up your personnel and you're not going to believe in your personnel, there's no use having no personnel! Even if your personnel is wrong inside of the prison, let the prisoner think that your personnel's right. Get the guard off to himself and tell him, says, "Now if that thing happens thataway again, handle it this away; you was wrong that time, handle this away. But, in the face of that prisoner, he thinks you was right 'cause I'm not going to tell you in front of a prisoner that you was wrong."

But the prisoner, he can tell you, you're telling a damn lie;

right there in the room, tell the guard that. That's the kind of discipline they got. Well that's the kind of discipline in my book that's no good. Whenever you violates your rules, if you'll take that strap right then, it'll get him straight—and then forget about it. You won't have near as much punishment, you won't have near as much bookkeeping to do, you just won't have as much trouble. Make your reputation!

All right, say you're a criminal, you and Fred, you're going in to Alabama and you're looking for some place to hold up or some place to break the law, you're going to take inventory to see how the penitentiary is before you do that. There's no question about it; that's common sense you're going to do that. 'Cause you might get caught, you say, "All right, they ain't very tough here in Alabama, so if we get caught we'll just go to the penitentiary and then tell them we don't know how to read and write and nothing like that, don't got no trade or nothing, and they'll sit us over there in the corner somewhere." So they pay you, they'll pay you to go to school. So, instead of—when you come in there I'd say, "I want you do so and so and so and so out yonder and dig that ditch." And you tell me you ain't going to do it and then I'd take force to whatever is necessary to put you in that ditch to put you to work. And then, when you come into Alabama, you took inventory and you said, "This here is a rough prison here; you'd better watch your business 'cause if you get caught here, it's hell." So then you'll go on down to Florida or somewhere else. It'll eliminate your criminals in Alabama.

'Course, like it stands now, it's over the United States that the prisoners is running them. Not only this one, all of them. I read it every day what they did. Whenever a bunch of prisoners can sit down and demand what they want to eat or how they want to work and get it—and what they want to wear—you hadn't got any penitentiary. You got a country club. You ain't got no penal system. It'd pay just as well over there to run all the guards off and just let the prisoners run it; that's what they're doing anyhow. The guards is just doing what the prisoners want done. It's a state farm over there, but they just don't work the farm. The farm's there, the prison's there, but the farm—there's nobody working it. Spending a bunch of money and not doing nothing.

Which, now my idea of penal systems could be wrong, but if you'll just think, they worked one time. If they worked one time, they'll work again. And I'm for this: if you got something working, there's no use changing it. 'Cause you might change it and it'll cost you thousands of dollars. If it's a running good, let it alone.

No, the prisoners ain't put the hat on the people, they just by gosh put the hat on the court and the president and everything under him—Congress and everything else. It would be the people, but I wouldn't put the average man in with it 'cause there's a bunch of people in this country that's really sick of that thing over yonder. That's the reason I put it in Washington, I put it on the big boy up there, 'cause they're the ones that's passing all the laws. And that United States Supreme Court, why they ought to be elected by the people, they ought not to be appointed up there and appointed for life! Know what I mean? That's one of the worst mistakes I think we got in our country.

My first day of retirement I felt like, when I woke up that morning, I'd been going to the prison every morning at four-thirty, and get up and go to the prison. Then I was there when they fed breakfast. I'd come back home and eat breakfast after they checked the prisoners out and fed them. So, that was after where I got to where I could retire, I'd worked up to deputy warden, I'll say that. 'Course when I was a guard I had to be there at daylight, take a bunch of prisoners, and I was there until dark. But whenever after I got up to deputy warden, then I could come back home and eat my breakfast. I didn't have to be there, but I was always there. If anything happened I'd be there to answer all the questions. That first morning I woke up—well I woke up at four-thirty for several mornings—I wanted to go over there, but I got up and went to doing something else and got my mind on it, and it wasn't but about two or three weeks 'fore it begin to wear off of me.

So now I don't even, the only thing I worry about now is just the condition the thing's in. It's in such bad condition, that worries me. I hate to see a thing as big as that, and was in as good as shape as it was one time, to get in the shape it's in now. I hate that.

But, in other words, I feel like I put my whole life in it and I felt like I was a part of it. So now there's no discipline, they don't work, letting the prisoners run it, so I don't go over there on that account.

There wasn't anything special when I retired. No, they didn't—they wrote me up in the Mobile paper and the Atmore paper and they put in a write-up about discipline, that I was a staunch discipline man, and I also told them that I believe prisoners working, helping support themselves, that I didn't think they ought to be a burden on the taxpayers. I also had a pamphlet wrote up and put it on the bulletin board up there, that if I had ever done anything or said anything to a guard that made him mad with me or anything, I done it for his benefit, that I didn't intentionally make him think that I was picking at him or anything like that. I says, "I've corrected a bunch of guards that I know got mad enough to fight me when I corrected them, but I was doing it for their own benefit." And I put a bulletin on the prison board down there that if I had ever punished a prisoner unjustly, that I didn't know it and I was sorry if I did and I hoped all of them was well, got their time made, and got out as quick as they could, and that I was retiring out of it.

Oh, yeah, there was a bunch of them. I can go out to that prison right now, go out there and in twenty minutes they'll be one walk up to me, say, "Why don't you come back over here and straighten this thing out?" These prisoners that's out on parole, built their time, and got a job here in Atmore, comes in the liquor store where my other son works and sees me, white and black, comes over and shakes hands with me and asks me how I'm getting along and all that, says, "Mr. Dees, they sure need you back out yonder at the prison," and all that sort of stuff, which makes me feel good. But I'm not any more physically shape to go back out there 'cause I couldn't take all that stuff they got out there now. They got that program that they don't work and all that land laying out and all them ditches filled up and all them prisoners laying inside and all them psychologists, psychiatrists, everything else walking around there and messing with it—I wouldn't fool with it.

A policeman is no better than his source of information, a sheriff is no better than his source of information, a warden is no better than his coooperation and his source of information, and you can't run a thing when you got four, five bosses telling you what to do; there's got to be a head to everything. The Lord didn't put but one head on every man, so there's somebody got to be in charge. Three or four can't be in charge, three or four can't give orders. One man has to give the orders and it has to go up and down the chain of command so everybody will know what's going on. If you don't, you blow it up.

2 FRED H. DEES, SR.

A road boss and former superintendent

describes the day-to-day existence of

road-camp inmates.

FRED DEES, SR.

JENNIE

(MRS. FRED DEES, SR.)

Fred and Jennie Dees were

secretly married as teenagers in the 1940s. He was an all-state high-school football player, the first in Atmore's history. She was a cheerleader who went to summer school so they could graduate together. They grew up in Southern family tradition: close to home. They have two daughters and a son, who also remain close to home. The eldest of the three is Fred, Jr., a probation officer working in a halfway house for parolees in Mobile.

For Fred and Jennie, raising a family within hearing distance of a convict road camp did not come easily.

Jennie: *"It was a matter of maintaining control. It was something that I knew I had to do. I knew I had to maintain that kind of control. And I respected Fred's ability to take care of situations, too. I never worried about what influence Fred's work would have on the children, for this reason. Fred was always able to make that kind of transition from prison warden to father by walking up the road. That was something that he had to do, and he was able to do that. Everything we've ever done was out in the open. We've never kept anything from Fred at all, in any area of our life."*

Fred: *"My kids never questioned me, my kids would be curious when I would be coming home, but Jennie taught them not to never question me. She taught them that if he wants you to know, you could know. And when I come home, I came out of one world into another.*

"Sometimes it was hard for me to make a change in that five-hundred and twenty-seven feet, that's how far it is from the front door of the camp to the front door of my house . . . and it was hard for me to walk away out of that and for me to be another person when I got to the house, and I appreciated Jennie teaching them not to be inquisitive.

"So, it was hard to explain how you feel. Maybe you got two, three drunks on your hands, and you got a guard who calls ten minutes before you check in and he's not coming, and then you have to make all the other arrangements and you maybe got one convict you got to get satisfied, and then on the other hand you got the Highway Department calling saying you got a hole out there on the road and you got to get out there and tend to it, and you got that on your mind, and you got a convict that's drunk on your mind, and you're trying to decide what you're going to do in each situation at the same time, and you walk right out of that and in five-hundred and twenty-seven feet you're home! And have a smile on your

face when you get in the door! And it was hard and Jennie helped me a lot in doing it."

Jennie: *"Sure, we discussed the children, a lot of times when they were little that when a disaster came, a major disaster—the Cuban crisis was a good example, had we been under attack for instance—Fred would have to be on his job; there would be no way he could be with his family, so it would be up to us to make whatever preparations necessary. We understood that, we recognized that fact, that he, even during the Hurricane Camille, Little Fred and Patty and I slept in the living room on the floor and on the couch. We were alone and we slept in the living room so we could be close to the telephone if Fred called. But that was just something that we all knew, and they grew up knowing that his first priority was his other family, the prisoners. My convictions are that children are individuals also. What they turn out to be in their life is not a result of what mother and daddy want for that particular person."*

Fred did not intend to become a prison man like his father. At first he worked for his father-in-law and then he became a butcher by trade. An argument with his boss and a timely job offer from prison officials led to a new career. The inmates called him Little Diesel, not because of his size—he's over six feet tall and more than two-hundred pounds—but in deference to his father. Convict respect for Oscar Dees transferred readily from him to his son. But, as generations change, so did the methods of prisoner treatment change with the second-generation prison man.

Fred: *"Daddy had to work with the convicts that I never come in contact with, . . . with the ones they had to keep locked up at all times. That's the ones that would kill you at a drop of the hat. Daddy, I guess, enjoyed his work, but now I really enjoyed what I did because I got to know each one of them as individuals. Things happened; you lived, you actually worked under tension because you never knew what one of them was going to do."*

The unforeseen was to eventually happen. Civil-rights issues were gaining momentum in the South, although at first they centered largely on integrating schools and obtaining voting rights. The prison system until then had been neglected. Fred was suspicious of the unpredictable convict, but he was not prepared in 1961 when a black prisoner accused him and another state employee of unlawful assault in an attempt to punish and obtain a confession—in effect, a charge that Fred had feloniously deprived the convict of his civil rights. There was a federal grand jury indictment, and Fred was suspended pending the outcome of the trial. *Specifically, Fred and his codefendant were accused of whipping the convict to make him confess to stealing a filing cabinet. The case went to trial in early October, 1962, in the federal district court in Mobile.*

Fred: *"At that particular time the civil-rights business was strong— it was hot and heavy. Even one of the jurors wanted to make an example out of us because of it. They said, 'Let's send them to the penitentiary to make an example of them and then no one else will do it.' "*

The trial lasted four-and-a-half days and at its conclusion the all-white male jury acquitted Fred and his codefendant.

Fred: *"It was the first time in Alabama anybody was ever tried for whupping a convict."* He paused for a moment and then he added, *"and it was the last time."*

An example had been made.

Jennie: *"For three years they pushed this thing, this official and his friends, and two of them died violent, very sad deaths. The other, the liquor agent, lost his job and became an alcoholic and for all practical purposes he died."*

Today, most of the Alabama road camps are closed, though some have been converted to work-release centers. Fred continues to work for the Highway Department as a superintendent over road crews that at times include ex-convicts.

Fred H. Dees, Sr.

One shed had dynamite in it, the other shed they had the fuses and the caps in it. So us boys would go up there, we'd dig a hole up underneath the building—wasn't nothing but dirt. So we would get us some dynamite caps and fuses and on the creek that ran up round the state farm, we'd go up there and dynamite it, cut the dynamite up into pieces and—you know, cut it up into little pieces like that, put a cap in it, fuse it like firecrackers, and throw it in the water. And when it would go off, it would kill the fish and they'd come to the top. Then we'd jump in the water and get the fish out.

What stopped it all was: the creek was pretty swift, so me and

another boy was going to get down there on a log and they'd
throw the dynamite in above us—we were just going to stay on
the log, you know. Shoot, my dynamite went off and it nearly
done floated down there on us. Boy did we get off of that log! We
quit that practice quick.

We would just do anything. At night, to pass the time off—
both sides of the highway went through the reservation, had pe-
can trees planted—so we'd go around there and get us some big
hunks of coal, and everybody's scared, you know, that's on that
prison farm, they'd drive straight down that road. The quicker
they got off, the better they'd feel. So, we would just drop that
coal on top of the car, and then run. If they'd stop, we'd climb
down and then run. One fellow caught us running and beat us
about half to death.*

When I was young the saying—a joke is what it was—was in
Atmore—we use to kid one another about going and getting a
Mennonite girl and marrying her because the whole community
chipped in and put you in the farming business. They'd buy you
a farm, a home, tractor, and give you about fifteen-hundred to
sixteen-hundred dollars to live on. The only thing was, they was
all ugly as sin!

Well, let's see, Daddy and Mother moved to Atmore prison
when I was two years old, and they had lived in two or three houses
there, but the only house I remember living in was the one where
the dogs was. And they kept, I imagine, anywhere from sixty to
hundred dogs at different times, right side of the house. And
we lived there until I was fourteen years old—we moved away
from there when I was fourteen. We moved to Atmore, and that's

---

*Oscar Dees: "I never did worry about him at all 'cause I just didn't feel
like they'd turn out to be that sort of boys. So, they didn't. 'Course I
never did have to punish them very much. I got a hold of them—the
worse time I ever got a hold of them—I caught them smoking behind
the garage and from then on they had enough respect for me, even
after they was all grown, they wouldn't smoke in front of me, they'd go
somewhere else and smoke and wouldn't let me see them smoking."

when daddy went to Birmingham to be warden of Ketona. Well, he had already been working up there about six months.

I went to school in Robinsonville, Alabama, a little ol' town up near the state farm. That was during the time Daddy was shot— I went to Robinsonville. I went to another little ol' school during the time that he was in the hospital getting over being shot. I went to this school that had six grades, first to the sixth, in one room. Had six rows of desks, and each row was first, second, third and fourth grade. One teacher for them all. Later we started going to school at Atmore. Shortly thereafter we moved to Atmore, and Daddy went to Birmingham.

When I was a boy we went to church. Regular. My mother took us. All the time, every Sunday. We started going to church when we was, I guess, six or seven years old. I joined the church when I was thirteen years old. That was the Baptist church. My daddy goes to the Baptist church now in Robinsonville. That's where his mother and daddy and all are buried, at Robinsonville Baptist Church. My mother and daddy will be buried there, too. Same graveyard.

There was twenty-nine of us boys in ages running from school age to seniors in high school that lived there on that state farm. Most of the time when you seen one of us you seen us all together. They was guards' kids, blacksmiths' kids, then there was the people that run the prison; they all lived on it. You take, I would imagine out of the twenty-nine, ten of them worked with the state. You see, the majority of them followed right along with their daddy working for the state.

We stayed together at school. We had the best baseball gloves, the best football and everything because, actually we got it from the prisoners. They would write to these associations and they would send you stuff. They was doing that back when I was a little boy. We rode the same school bus and we stayed pretty much to ourselves at school. All of us run together, you might say, and if somebody jumped on one of us, they had to whup us all. We looked out for one another. Which actually, that was taught to us by the convicts. Stick together. You know a convict is like that, they stick together.

Yeah, we'd just go up there and borrow the baseball or football equipment from the convict that had it in charge; we could just go up there and get it and carry it to school with us and play with it. We actually played ball with the convicts; the oldest ones was on the baseball team. Like, the city of Atmore had a baseball team and it was some of the boys was so good playing baseball that they would play on the team as convicts. They would go in there and dress out in a uniform. They was on the convict team!

There was two pitchers, two brothers, good baseball pitchers, and they pitched for the prison team. The visiting team never knew it, they never did know if they was convicts or not! The town team, they gathered up the best baseball players they could find, too, and brought them down. They had a referee, a guard was the referee. But they was hard losers, they played to win. They wouldn't raise sand or nothing like that, but it was just like a baseball game that you see on television. They had the right to say, "Referee, you were wrong, you made a mistake." They would throw a fit, you know, throw their hat on the ground, just like on television. But when it was all over with, they left the baseball field. It was all in fun.

They had some good baseball teams. I never was old enough to play. We was away before I got old enough to play with them. But now, whenever they had a practice, they let us all play; we all practiced with them. We practiced with them all the time— take batting practice, such as that.

Now, I wasn't counting the girls. Well, the girls had to stay home and sew! Another thing, the girls couldn't travel very good, you know, amongst the convicts. Us boys, we could go, but the girls, they had to stay at home; they couldn't go nowhere, they had to stay inside. At night, there was always somebody giving a party, so many families there; it was always somebody's birthday, which we would get together at night for a birthday party or something like that.

And then they would shake the convicts in, they had Little River State Park, which the CCC boys built way back yonder in the Depression. Little River State Park. And they would take the truck that they would use to haul the dogs and the horses around for the escaped convicts and three times a week, I believe it was, we would all meet up there, boys and girls, and they'd carry all us to Little River and we'd go swimming, maybe three, four times a week.

There was always something going on. Like Momma, they quilted back then all the time, and during the day all the ladies was gathered up somewheres at somebody's house. We was running around there, into ever'thing. Then after we got older, us boys went fishing and hunting all the time. Or selling all the scrap iron we could pick up! Stealing the state's peaches and selling them! Syrup, and sell it!

We had a key to everything. They didn't lock us boys out; them convicts could make a key to anything. When we wanted a key made we just told them go make us a key for such and such a lock and they'd do it! We would use the horses, wagons, everything. We had, actually, more to entertain us than the people outside the state property because we had so many different things that we could do.

But, now the girls were different. They didn't go walking in the woods or walking up the road like us 'cause their mothers and daddies wouldn't let them. But you could get up in the morning when I was a boy—shoot, we would get up and play and rouse around everywhere, come back about dinner time and eat dinner and we'd be gone again! Until dark. Mules and horses, they had mules and horses running out their ears! In the morning some of us boys, the youngest, would go up there when they caught the mules to plow every day, we'd go up there and maybe ride the mules back to where they was going to work that day, and we'd walk back and then about the time they would knock off for dinner we'd be back out there where we could ride the mules back in. Just like I say, you had something to do all the time.

The trusties, they went inside to eat most of the time, but a lot of the times they done their own cooking. They cooked bread for the dogs—to feed the dogs—and that bread was cooked by a special cook, which to keep the convicts from putting some poison or something in it, and they had to cook beef all the time for the dogs and they had them a pot out there and they'd make

their own stew and such as that. And during the spring of the
year and the summer when everything was—vegetables was in—
they done a lot of their own cooking out there. They done it
outside; they didn't have no stove or anything like that. And
naturally, me and my brother, we ate with them! Always better.

No, my mother didn't worry about us 'cause actually there
wasn't nothing to hurt us. The convict wasn't going to hurt us.
It was so much different back then than it is now. It's hard to explain. You never heard of a convict sassing a guard, you never
heard of nothing like that. And when a convict run, he stayed in
the woods, he was scared to get out and let anybody see him 'cause
he was afraid somebody would kill him.

Now, any convict, shoot, he—you know they just tried two for
raping two of the girls on state-farm property up there in the
last two weeks. Sure did, tried them two weeks ago. Two weeks
ago. From Atmore prison. This particular one was a trusty. He
raped one, but he had both of them—he kidnaped both of them.
Left both of them in the woods when he left. He run whenever
he left; he left in a truck and they caught him, after he committed
the crime.

I think the most frightening thing that ever happened to me—
I had a paper route and the people that lived on the farm, I de-
livered the papers to them, to the house, and then the ones that
lived away from up there, I would go there to the gate where
they checked the convicts in and wait for them there and give
them the papers. So, I was sitting there one evening, on the bench.
There was a shed to one side, the building where they kept the
guns at. On the other side was where the guards stayed that operated the gate. And they had a squad of men—a squad run anywhere from twenty men to fifty—but this squad that they had
had about twenty-five in it, and when they was shaking them
down they grabbed the guard, and when they grabbed the guard
he didn't have no gun, but he hollered for the guard that was
standing outside, that had the gun, to shoot them. And he did.
I got up under the bench. They killed one and wounded three
more. That scared me to death. Shotgun. They was going to hold

the guard for hostage. They didn't figure the guard would shoot, them having a hold of him.

'Course all the prisoners knew who we were, too. And if we had a gun with us, we could go hunting, but we'd carry a trusty convict with us. That was to keep somebody from taking the gun away from us. The trusty was supposed to been picked out to where he wouldn't do anything like taking a gun away from us. It was an honor for him to walk around with kids, you know, and the kids toting a gun, he could go as far as he wanted to. When my gun got heavy, I let him tote it.

I imagine there was six or seven, maybe eight, trusties worked and lived down there. They had a little house back of our house that they slept in. The reason they slept in it was because they had caught so many escaped convicts that they felt like it was dangerous for them to sleep inside the prison, and they let them sleep outside. Even when I was young, to go hunting or fishing, one of them always went with us, which was to keep the convicts, if they was to escape, from messing with us. He was sent with us. We thought it was 'cause he just wanted to go, but in later years we found out it was for our protection.

Even riding horses, which we had, we could go get a horse any-time we wanted to, providing we carried one of the dog boys—is what they called them—carried one of them with us. We could go anywhere we wanted to on the state farm property, providing we carried one with us. I never was scared of them. Back then Mother and Daddy would go visiting maybe for a weekend, and my younger brother and I, Dale, we wouldn't want to go, and one would stay in the house with us. We had a cook, we had a dog boy, and then there was a yard boy and then there was the cook. And the yard boy done the cleaning of the house, ironing for mother; and the cook, he cooked. All of them was trusties, and they would stay there if we didn't want to go with Momma and Daddy; we'd just stay there, and they'd stay with us. All blacks. I imagine Atmore was fifty/fifty back then, but they was seg-regated—they had the black cells and the white cells. They kept them segregated. The only—Daddy had to have a few white men working down there, but as far as any of them getting close to us kids, we never messed with the white; most of the time they was black.

On the days that they wasn't working you could go up there; we could get a horse if we wanted to, and ride. In the wintertime they took the mules and put them in a pasture in the woods. That was the biggest pasture. We would go over there and catch the mules and ride them. But you got throwed a pretty good bit over there. Gosh, they're hard to ride.

When I was a kid they didn't have nothing but mules—that's all they plowed with. Then they come up, the first tractors they had—I was pretty good sized boy when they brought the first tractors. And the only thing they did with them was to break land. They'd break the land up, then they'd take a mule and plant it and cultivate it.

We went all over the place. They would let us inside the prison in the daytime, but now at daytime all your men was out in the field, except your trusties. We could go all through the prison in the daytime; but now at night, whenever they checked back in, they wouldn't let us in there.

Then there was the old convicts. I was so small—maybe they might have had a stroke, but anyway they was unable to work. They let them live in a little ol' house right back there of the cold storage, which there wasn't very many; I'd say the most ever stayed there was ten, maybe fifteen. That was one of the places we were forbidden to go because Daddy told us not to play in there because you'd catch bedbugs or lice or something like that. Also, we was forbidden to play on the mattresses when they was sunning them. They sunned them every two months, something like that. And we was forbidden from playing on those too, but we did, and when we got caught they'd wash us down in sulfur when we got home to kill the bedbugs and the lice and everything we might have picked up. They wouldn't even let us come in the house until they did it. Daddy would always see us. He was over there all the time around the prison. He would catch us playing

on them; that's when they would send us home and tell Momma
we'd been playing on the mattresses. I don't know if there was
any bedbugs on them or not, but I guess it was for them to take
that kind of precaution when they caught us playing on them.
He had convicts that would tell on us, just like he had convicts
that told on the other convicts! They would tell on us, too.

We moved from the prison, out to the house in Atmore. When
we moved there, Daddy was in Birmingham. For the first two
years, maybe three years, we lived at Atmore, we had a prisoner
that stayed with us, doing the housework. We had fixed the
garage up behind the house, and he lived there; it was an apart-
ment really. And he lived there and he cooked breakfast every
morning; he'd wake us up, get us off to school or work, whichever one.

In the summer time we worked. But we had one there, us boys,
we didn't have to do none of the yard work or toting the coals or
nothing like that, and we used him for a playmate, too. He played
ball with us and all. Then he would whup us when it was necessary, too. If we did anything wrong while Momma was at work,
he'd whup us just like Momma would. And when Mother would
come he would tell Mother what we had did, that he had whupped
us, and most of the time she would whup us again! He was black.
And if we did something with him that was wrong, Momma would
whup him along with us, too. She would use a switch, a belt. Which
he was young—he was a young convict. I doubt if he was over
nineteen years old whenever he started working for us. He came
back to see us. He made parole, and then after he made parole
Momma never did want another one. Oh, I guess four or five
years after he got out he came back to see us all. Just like part of
the family, you know, living with him like that. The best I remember he was either working at the house or he was helping with
the dogs out there at Atmore. I don't remember exactly what he
was doing, but we had known him before we went in to town.

He was called a house boy. Everybody that, I think above a
guard, back then, had a house boy. Which he was a lot of fun. He
would tell us big tales about this and that. Taught us how to gamble, how to cuss. We looked up to him, we thought he was big.

He'd tell me to look out for him. He had a girl friend he'd go see.
He'd slip off and go see her 'cause Momma wouldn't give him
permission to go. And he was supposed to stay there at the house
all the time, but he'd tell me he was going and if something happened and we needed him, Mother would always send me to go
get him and I had to go out there to get him. And if he wasn't
there I'd come back and tell Momma he was sick or something
like that, that he'd be there after a little while. And he'd cover for
us. But if we did, especially me, if I did anything Mother would
get real mad about, he would have to tell Momma about that.
Specially things like, if she told us to do something, or help him
do something, she wanted us to work, more or less to have something to occupy our time, too. Maybe she'd tell me to rake the
leaves and when I got home he would tell me, "Ol' Miz told you
to rake the yard, now if you don't rake them you know she's going
to be mad when she gets home and she's going to whup us all."
And, naturally me being a boy and all I'd say, "Well, I'll do it if
you'll come and help me," and naturally he'd go and help and
he'd tell Momma I'd done it when she got home. He'd done 90
percent of it!

    Two years before I ever started working for the state, the peo-
ple that knew Daddy, which they knew me, that was in charge
of hiring personnel, had been after me. Every time I'd go visit
Daddy they would try to hire me to work, and I never really
thought about working for the state. Fact of the matter, they
offered me a job one time and I told them I'd take it, then I turned
it down. I was working with Jennie's daddy at that time.
    But now when I went to work with the state, which I'm a butcher
by trade, and that's what I was doing in a grocery store, and I
was working in Atmore in a grocery store with a man that I had
worked for when I was going to high school. And him and I had
had a disagreement this particular morning, and the man which
was over the road camps called me about an hour after then, and
I was all mad and didn't much care then—young you know—
and he offered me a job in Grove Hill, and I told him I'd take it.
And I reported up there the next day. That was in 1952. I was
twenty-two years old.

My first job classification called for steward. That's what they called you. But you kept books and also looked after the cleaning and the cooking in the convict camp. Which was the same as a deputy warden—they just had a different name for it. I stayed there until January, 1958, then I was transferred to Loxley, and I stayed down there until May of '58. Then I went back to Grove Hill, and I was transferred in April of '61 to Eight Mile; I can tell you the months.

All right, I started in Grove Hill August the 27th, 1952. I got transferred in January of 1958 to Loxley and I was transferred back to Grove Hill May the 7th of 1958. April the 16th I was transferred to Eight Mile and then I worked at Eight Mile until, February the 28th, I was transferred to the First Division, which is the north section of Alabama, and I worked up there six weeks and then I got laid off—no I worked up there a little longer—I got laid off in April. I believe it was the 15th of April that I got laid off. Then I stayed off then until I was tried and I went back to work on October the 16th of 1962. Now, those were all road camps. Later, after the trial, I was eventually transferred to Eight Mile, where I stayed until after they closed it.

The Highway Department rented the road-camp convicts from the Board of Corrections. Each district in a division had a convict camp, and the Highway Department hired the personnel to run each convict camp, and the superintendent or warden— he was called either one; the Board of Corrections called him the warden, the Highway Department gives you the title of superintendent of that road camp or district. He's superintendent of a district, of so many miles of road. Well, the superintendent is the go-between for the Board of Corrections and the Highway Department. In other words, he had to answer to two departments; he had to answer to the Board of Corrections for the welfare of the convicts, and then he had to answer to the Highway Department about the work on the highways. He had two sets of bosses with the Board of Corrections and the Highway Department. The Highway Department paid him, but he had to satisfy both departments.

Our only personnel was Highway Department, but the Board

of Corrections set out the rules to govern them by. They set out
the rules to govern the convicts, such as visiting, who visited, all
the rules of handling them were set by the Board of Corrections.
Which is the same rules they used in the big penitentiaries. They
were identical. I was the only one who had to answer to the Board
of Corrections. The guards had to answer to me. When the Board
of Corrections wanted to know anything they talked direct to
me. On anything to do with a convict, the superintendent of the
road camp had to deal with the Board of Corrections. Like the
doctors and the bills and such as that, the Board of Corrections
paid it, and I had to handle all that. Even the resident engineer
who is over me—that's the next step in the system—he had no
say-so over the road camp. He had a say-so over what they did,
the work that they did, he told me what kind of work he wanted
and when. He set out a schedule for me to go by, really, and when
I caught on the schedule I had to still work the convicts, which I
would have to find work for them to do, which was very easy.
The main thing in a road camp, there's so much to do. But you
was really in a road camp. Now, when I first started working we
had a few county convicts, but the county has to handle their own
convicts.

The superintendent was kind of his own boss; you could always
get by. If you didn't want to ride all day behind his crews you
could "need" to go to Atmore to pick up some clothes—one thing
or another. You could just go. You done just about like you wanted
to, but you still had a lot of responsibility; nobody else could take
it off you. It was your responsibility. It caused you to work long
hours because you was the doctor, the daddy, the mother, and
everything 'cause they had to be on the road all day. And the
mail would come in, which during camp you had to censor the
mail, that was another thing I bypassed down here; I told them
that if they would be good, I would not even censor their mail.
The only thing I did, I made them open the mail in front of the
guard in case that the folks sent them money, that I could make
a record of it, 'cause you run into a lot of things—they would write
a letter saying, "I am sending you some money," and the money
wouldn't be in there. Cause a pretty good stink, you know—that
the guards was taking the money and all that—and I tried to
avoid all that I could, but it was a lot of fun. They'd get their

mail and their brother was sick, or their momma was sick or their daddy was sick and no guard down there had the authority to call any of the people—I handled all that, and I'd come home and by the time I'd get home they'd call and ol' so-and-so wants to talk to you, and I'd have to go back down there and talk to him, and if it was necessary I'd contact his people.

That causes a lot of your trusties to escape. He gets a letter from his wife that his daughter is real sick or expecting to die or something and the people paints the worst picture. When they write, I'm not trying to say they tell stories, but actually—their husband's in the penitentiary and she feels like she's got all the responsibility, the child, and when she sits down to write him about it she paints it darker than it really is.

They used to tell the new convicts about me—well, a new convict would come in and I talked to every one of them. If I wasn't at the camp when they got them, nobody fooled with them until I got there, and I went over my rules and regulations. Every warden or superintendent's got his own rules and regulations, too, along with the ones the Board of Correction sets up. Well, I tried to be as nice to them and I smiled about 90 percent of the time, and they would be up there and they would go back and tell the old convicts that was there, you know, "Captain Dees is a nice fellow, he smiles, laughs all the time." And they'd say, "Yeah, yeah, don't you get fooled by that smile."

Let me back up. I worked under Mr. Simpson up yonder, when I started work. I worked under him for nine years and naturally everybody's got their own ideas; I knew that sooner or later I would run a convict camp. I knew that, in other words, I was offered one way before I ever accepted one. And I—Mr. Simpson ruled with a firm hand; he was—didn't use as much force as a lot of them did, but he believed in force. He was the superintendent and I was a bookkeeper under him, and I had it in my mind that I would run a camp without any force. To put it plain, I thought I could outsmart a convict. But I was wrong. You can outsmart a certain percent of them, and a certain percent of them got more sense than you got.

I made my own reputation. Convicts who knew me when I was a boy tried to treat me as a boy. Convicts that been under Daddy

would be sent to a road camp and they had it in their head that
by their serving time under my father and now under me that I
would lighten up on them a little, you might say. They used to
try to put the hat on me; they like to try to put the hat on me in
the respect about how good a convict man my daddy was. And I
would tell them quick, I would say, "Well, Daddy runs his and I
run mine," and I said, "Now if you want to know what I'll do you
just try me." But I guess I got by a lot of times on Daddy's reputation. You could say that and be honest, that I got by a lot of times
on his reputation.

I think that the best convict man is a man that'll think like a
convict. In other words, if he can get down on the same ground
that the convict's on.

One of the best convict men the state of Alabama ever had was
a man named William Carlson. He called me "son." At the time
I went to work for the state he was over the classification division,
which he classified fifty convicts out that went to road camps.
Well, he would have one that William Carlson knew was—if
anybody could ever get his attention—that he would work out.
And he would sent him to these different road camps and they
would never work out, and he'd get him and he'd call me up,
say, "Son," (I'd say, "Yes, sir"), "I'm going to send you ol' Charlie
Rickmon," or whatever his name was (but Charlie Rickmon was
one in particular); he said, "Fred, he's all right if you can get his
attention!" So, I knew right then when he walked in the door you
were supposed to knock him down! Discipline is a certain amount
of fear.

Now, the guard that really and truly got along with the convicts
better than anybody I ever seen was Cotton. That was his nickname. Cotton was—he couldn't see; he couldn't recognize a
man twenty-foot ahead of him. This was when he was older. He
worked for me about six years during the time Eight Mile Camp
was coming to a close, but I felt more at ease at night with Cotton
down there than I did with someone that could see because the
convicts had more respect for him than any guard, and he had
two or three that would look out for him.

It was just like when they hit the steel for bed count, they counted
for him, they did his job for him. And if two of them was fighting,

they'd separate them for him. It's just 'cause they had a lot of respect for him. Cotton wasn't mean, but he didn't take no junk now. He wouldn't let them run over him. He was fair-minded, really, very, very fair-minded. He's sixty-eight years old now. He was in his sixties then. He didn't have no gun or anything. You had to bear in mind, down there we didn't have no guns. At night, whenever they were pulling the bed, they had guards to walk in case of fire or anything, or if one got sick or one tried to kill another one, he was there to stop that—he was there more to protect the convict than he was to guard him.

Instead of a gun they'd use a walking stick. Made out of hickory; it will get the job done. That's an attention stick, too.

I had one foreman that was just the opposite. Now, he was the kind of fellow who dearly loved to punish a convict. Oh, he put hell on a convict. If he had a new convict, say, check the new one out too, he would load him up on the truck and when he got him away from the camp he would make the driver stop the truck and tell another one to get the tarpaulin and lay it down on the ground and tell the new convict to lay down there, and he'd whup out his knife, and naturally the convict bawled, "Boss, what you want, what you want, what's the matter." "I'm going to kill you, you ol' goddamn son of a bitch, I don't like your damn looks. Reason I want you on that tarpaulin when I kill you I'm going to wrap you up and drop you in the Mobile River."

That's the kind he was, I didn't go for that; I dearly hated him, I hated him. Which him and I had several run-ins, which I'll be frank exactly, I'll tell you word for word I told him. And I'll tell you what he told me. He put his hand in his pocket after his knife and I told him he could pull it out if he wanted to, that he would never eat a bar of candy that was going to be as sweet as that knife was going to be because I was damn sure going to make him eat it. He started out with the knife and I said, "Now I'm going to tell you the damn truth, I've got a gun in my pocket and I'm going to shoot the living hell out of you." And then he come out with this, saying, "Why, why don't you pick on somebody your size." Like a child, you see. I had done whupped him down.

He hated me too; it worked both ways. He was on the superintendent's list and had been working longer than I had, and he honest to God thought he should be the boss man. And he just,

he hated me because I had the job. And I hated him because he
mistreated convicts.

Reason he didn't get ahead was he was stupid. He didn't know
that. He had no personality—let's get to the back of it all. He had
no personality; his attitude was wrong for the job. Control convicts by fear. And no reason about it, you couldn't reason with
him at all. Which ever'body in the state, you know, he had been
called for several interviews, but nobody was no fool. He wanted
to be the 'gator. Let me get the word right. In a penitentiary a
bad convict we referred to him as a 'gator, and the guards, the
meanest guards, when the convict talked about him, they talked
about him as the 'gator. Well, his nickname was Daddy Bad,
that's what the convicts called him—Daddy Bad. And he wanted
to live up to his reputation, as he called it, of being rough and
bad. But I didn't go for that stuff.

The easiest three years that I ever run a convict camp was the
road camp here at Eight Mile. I was lucky and got about 70 percent of the population interested in making money on the side
and I in turn told them that I would let them make their little
lamps and billfolds. I even went as far as to help finance them,
and as long as they obeyed the rules, the ones that was set out by
the Board of Corrections and the ones I set out to operate the
camp with, that I would just let them stay up at night, a reasonable
time, and I would let them keep the tools where they would be
handy to them where they wouldn't have to check them in and
out. And as long as it kept them occupied like while they was
inside the camp, I could have left Rover down there and he could
have took care of them. A few you had didn't care, but the ones
who wanted to outnumbered them, and they kept the others
straight.

The superintendent himself had to do the banking for them,
that was his responsibility. For every inmate. No limit on the
amount. The most that I ever had was fourteen thousand dollars.
Kept it in a checking account. So where you had it to get it whenever you wanted it. The largest amount that a prisoner could
keep on hand? Well, the rules and regulations said five dollars,
but in a road camp it was whole lots. Depends on the superin-

tendent, how much he would let him have. He would buy leather, and resell and such as that. And you always got a loan shark in the prison, too. He's the one that had most of the money, he— for instance, say a man was in the penitentiary and his folks would save for two weeks and get him up a new pair of shoes, new underwear, and buy him all kinds of shaving stuff, and whenever they left he would pawn it to the shark, where he could gamble it. Well, the stuff that his people—like his shoes—when visiting Sunday would come, he couldn't get it out, he would pay the shark fifty cents extra to wear his shoes on visiting Sunday. The shark, he controlled the money, and he made the money. Interest was two bits on the dollar, twenty-five cents on the dollar.

We also went to several places and played baseball.* I even got to where I had to play with them. That was at Grove Hill. And they followed their own team just like you and I, they pulled for the teams of their choice. But, the best I remember, most of them was for the Dodgers, the majority of them were. And football was the Cleveland Browns. When they watched a game on television, we would have to calm them down more then than we did any other time. They'd get in arguments. But that kind of argument, there was never anything to it. It was just you and I would argue over a game of checkers or something like that; it never meant much.

Now that baseball team we had, it was a lot of fun. To get equipment you could write to some different people, we would con them. Like baseball equipment, that was the most easiest stuff to come by. You would set down and take a baseball and get the address on it, or a baseball bat or glove and get the address off the box, and get a convict and tell him how to go about conning them and you could get just all kinds of baseball equipment! That's where we got all the baseballs. You might be thinking of one or two, but I'm talking in terms of gross! You would write and tell them that you were in prison and you're interested in

---

*Jennie: "Fred had the first band in a road camp and he had a baseball team—before he became a superintendent."

baseball and you followed that team all the time and they don't
have no ways of getting baseballs and you was wondering if—you
see them on television throw so many baseballs away—that you
would be so glad to have some of the baseballs that they threw
away! And in a couple of weeks you would get a box loaded with
baseballs!

It's just like when I had them occupied doing things; we would
con 90 percent of the material that they worked with. We would
con it out of people. They would make lamps out of real thin
panel, and you could go to most any supply company and they'd
have a design and they'd have four or five sheets of it and you'd
tell that sad story and—"Oh, yeah, you can have it." And you
could get all that stuff.

I was known as the most conning superintendent that they
had! Like right on the road I would find this watermelon patch.
This man has growed to sell. Well, he can't sell them all because
after July everybody got watermelon then, so you go talk to him
about the time when he's done pulled about all he's going to pull,
you tell him you've got a convict camp and they ain't had no wa-
termelons that year and you were wondering if you might, before
he disced the land, that you might come out there and get a little:
"Oh, yeah, be glad to." Shoot, you'd just haul watermelon by the
load! Irish potatoes, you could go to Baldwin County and con
those potato sheds out of Irish potatoes.*

I had this highway-patrol officer conned because I would tell
him, "You get called to a wreck where a cow's involved, if you'll
get me there as quick as you can, we'll dress it," 'cause the stock
law keeps a man from owning a cow. In other words, if his cow
gets out and a car runs over it, he's foolish to say "It's mine" because if he says "It's mine" he has to buy an automobile. But anyway he would call and I would run get the cow and come and
dress it. I had a walk-in cooler and all and we'd hang it up in there,

---

*Jennie: "Well, if someone found a dead cow on the road—this always
fascinated me—someone who hit a cow on the road, the state troopers
always called Fred to come and move the cow out of the road and he'd
bring the cow up here, and they'd butcher it, and all the prisoners would
have steaks for supper!"

and when it got ready I would call him to come by and get his meat (I would always give him a hindquarter off it), and we'd eat the rest of it—when I say "we," I mean the crew and the convicts because we *all* feast!

And I had one place—Mabel's—which is a noted restaurant here in Mobile, one of the oldest restaurants in Mobile—well it's not in Mobile, it's in Coden, out of Mobile—but I had a deal with her. On her seafood, she always served fried chicken with it. She just used the good parts; the backs, the wings, and such as that she just kept them for me, and I would patch a hole or two in her driveway and give her a wheelbarrow full of oyster shells or something like that. We would average getting a hundred pounds a month of chicken backs and such as that, and chicken went good in mixing in your menu, you see.

And fish, I was lucky enough to have several convicts who would get in and get out, and they would work on the shrimp boats or fish boat. I kept in contact with them, put a little pressure on them, and we had a lot of fish and such as that. And then the supervisors in Montgomery—naturally when a convict goes back up there he'd put the word out, "Go back down there to Captain Dees to eat." Everybody said I could con folks out of stuff.

Now, salt pork was the most common meal they had. They had it at breakfast time, at lunch and dinner, both. Supper, whichever you want to call it. It was the cheapest meat you could buy in the meat markets and they fed a lot of it. Actually, at Kilby prison they butchered their own hogs and they made their own salt pork. Way back yonder they did that at Atmore, but here in the later years they did all the butchering at Kilby; they had a butcher shop there.

The convicts called salt pork Mississippi Catfish and Tennessee Chicken. Mississippi Catfish is when you boil it and take the salt out of it and you put meal on it and you fry it. Tennessee Chicken is the same but you put flour on it and fry it. Convicts named it. That's the only people I've ever heard call it that.

A typical work day? Well, say at Eight Mile Camp I'd be at the camp at five-thirty in the morning and, which you would check your breakfast for your men. They got up at five-thirty, the convicts I'm talking about, and they fed them at six. They had breakfast at six and you would naturally be in and out around that, you know, 'cause to see if there was any problem or anything. And then the foremans would start coming in about anywheres between six-thirty and seven and you would start instructing them, assigning them their duties for this particular day and whereabouts they would work and what you wanted them to do. These are the foremans for the road crews. And then at seven-thirty you would do what we call "check out," which is hit the steel and get all your convicts out there and they would have their lunch box—each lunch box would already be prepared for their dinner.

Midday. It would always be beans and bread, or peas and bread, but you would always give them something different. In other words, beans and bread was the regular dinner. You had beans and bread every day, but then sometimes you put baloney with it, white meat with it, cheese with it, and you just rotated different stuff like that to go with the beans. They would be hot whenever they carried them out. They carried them out in what they called—it was a milk pail is what it's called—and then what they'd do out there about ten o'clock, they'd build a fire and put a bucket of water on the fire, and they'd set the bucket of beans over in the water and that would get them hot for dinner. Lima beans, black-eyed peas, navy beans, kidney beans, you had all, you had about five or six; any kind of beans you name, we had them. Let's see, we had large and small lima, black-eyed peas, kidney beans, navy beans, and we had what they call a split-eye pea, which was a dry pea like a black-eye pea, but it was a small pea. Which now, you had canned string beans, you had them too. You could send corn—I have sent corn out there.

But you had to watch what you sent out there. Say if you cooked pork and macaroni, or pork and rice, that's a good one, you couldn't do that unless it was a certain time of the year. In the summertime, if you sent pork and rice out there it would sour and make them sick, and one of your main jobs—you had to just continuously check on it—is the containers that you sent that food out there with, 'cause you had to make the foremans be sure that when they got through eating that they would wash them as best as they could out there. Then when they was brought back inside, even though they might be clean looking, you had to be sure that they scalded them out in hot water to keep them from making them sick.

They had an hour off. And then during the time they left the camp until they came back in, and checking-in time would be five o'clock, so it would be five. You would check out at seven and come back in at four, and an hour for dinner, which the time that you checked in and out they changed all during the year on account of your sun. In other words, you would work eight hours. During the wintertime you'd leave at seven and in the summertime you'd leave at eight and you'd be back in at five and in the winter time you'd check out at seven and be back in at four. Daylight-saving time controlled that, too. And then while they was on the road your job was to go from crew to crew and check on the work and see if they was working all right, or doing right. And then in your rounds if you had any complaints about any kind of condition on the road from the public—maybe a man called in about his driveway or wanted a driveway or had a pipe stopped up, your job was to check on it, too. That's to line your work up for the next day; you scheduled to do all that kind of work.

And another thing, working in a highway, in the middle of a highway, you always got a smart SB, you know, that's in a hurry. And he comes flying up there and you got a convict flagging. Well to hell with that convict in his mind, you know. So the convict won't get out of his way and he has to stop. Well he stands and cusses the convict. Now, I have come close to killing somebody that way. And the guards, too. We dearly hate that kind of people. Because he's not doing nothing but taking advantage of that convict 'cause the convict can't protect himself.

Let's see, when I went down there to Eight Mile it was forty-two convicts. They had four crews. But at that particular time they was working—you always kept your flunkies, which was seven, six or seven, you had one that worked your guard, and then they had two or three that worked around the division office and, best I remember, maybe one maybe two that worked at the sign shop; then the rest of them was divided up in your road crew, whichever. You divided them up according to what each one had to do, his need for ever how many men, and then. But now we got the camp up later on to—I had eighty men one time down there and I had seven crews then—and when they closed it I only had four crews. The populations had done dropped back down to where you just had four crews.

When they came in from work they had to all take a bath, you had to see that each one took a bath, which he had clean clothes to put on, what we called his cell clothes, clothes he wore while he was inside the camp. They always wore what they called "free-world shoes" then. They worked in the state-issued shoes and then he would have a pair he bought or his folks brought him or he beat out of another one or something like that, or a pair of sandles—a lot of them wore sandles, shower sandles, about the majority of them wore them, especially in the summertime. They had to take a bath, and then we fed the supper about six, and they had from six until eight thirty to write letters or make bill-folds or watch television, play cards, or he could go to bed. It was his choice.

Mail call was every day. The mail came in in the morning and the superintendent or the bookkeeper had to read it and then— if no money came in the mail, money order or cash money, or a package—we let the hall man give the mail out. Now, any money or package, he had to sign to get it; you did that to clear yourself. In other words, if you was there and your momma sent you a dollar and just stuck it in a letter, you could get the letter and the next morning tell me you got a letter and somebody stole your dollar and you couldn't—assuming you didn't have no way to— go about proving what happened. So what you do if you got a dollar, you write his name down and one dollar in cash money and that night when he got his letter you make him sign for it; then you have a record that he got his money.

After they had supper, the mail was given out. For some of them it was important. Some of them never did get any.

But, now at eight-thirty we put them all to bed unless it was something on television they might want to watch to nine, and we would let the ones stay up if they had been quiet during the night, no trouble or nothing. Which program they watched was left entirely up to them. We let them argue it down to which program they watched, and if they got into too big an argument we cut it off and told them to go to bed. That's to keep them from arguing about it the next night. But they all liked pretty well the same thing. They watched all the baseball games, they watched all the football games, basketball games, and they would watch programs like *The FBI*. They like that, and any programs that had niggers on it. They watched all of them, and let's see what program—*Bonanza,* now they always watched *Bonanza*. On Sunday nights, that amazed me; and Lawrence Welk the musical show, they always watched it. Best I remember, it came in back then on a Thursday night. And they watched movies, they all liked movies; that's when you let them sat up to see the end of a movie, if it was a good one. They didn't watch them all, but we'd let them do it.

Now bedtime was eight-thirty Monday, Tuesday, Wednesday, and Thursday nights, but now on a Friday, Saturday, Sunday night I let them stay up 'til ten o'clock, which was my rules; the rules from Montgomery said eight-thirty, but I stretched it around a little bit. You kind of left that up to your hall man; that's the way he had of keeping the noise down so much during the night. The hall man would be the guard that was inside with them. When they went to bed they was locked up then and wouldn't be unlocked until the next morning. The cells, each cell was locked up. There was sixteen in each cell. The cell was ten-feet wide and forty-eight feet long.

Now, they had a saying, as free men meaning on the outside, one of them told me that if I could ever be a nigger for one Saturday night, I would never want to be anything else but a nigger again!

Saturdays and Sundays they didn't work. They didn't do any work around the camp, not really. Most, some of them, worked for themselves. He'd build lamps, make pocketbooks, such as that. Every other Sunday was visiting day.

No, the prisoners were never chained. They couldn't work

with that. The closest to them ever being chained would be when they would be brought down there, they would be chained then. Brought from the prison. From the "R and C" unit—the receiving and classification unit. Whenever they put them in a dogwagon they are handcuffed in that dogwagon and which there's a chain that goes through the handcuffs. They're sitting them just like a bus but the seats are not crossways—it's down the side; and then it had a double seat down the middle of it, and each one of them had a chain that hooked in one end, and it come through handcuffs and locked back down into the seat and just run a chain through the handcuffs. And it was one of their rules that every man who rode it had to be handcuffed. No matter whether he was a trusty or not, that was the rule that everybody who rode in that dogwagon had to be handcuffed.

Well they always used a bus, but they used a bus same as a Greyhound bus, but they had it barred up and everything. The dogwagon was the vehicle they used to transfer prisoners. All over the state. That they picked up from the jails, that they carried in and then carried them back out, transferred them between Kilby to Atmore and then to the road camps. Which they had several of them. They had a big one like the Greyhound bus, and then they had smaller ones. It's according to—if they, for instance, if they would just go and pick up two prisoners they had a pickup fixed like that. And then if they was going to haul fifty or sixty they'd use that big bus. And every one of them was called a dogwagon. Now, where they got that name, Lord knows.

And I had sick call every night after we got through eating. I would just ring—what we call "hit the steel"—which it's nothing but a bell that you just hit it and you get their attention. You just holler out "sick call" and then all of them that was sick or wanted any kind of medicine would come up there and we would issue it out to him if we thought he needed it; if we didn't, we didn't do it.

It was left entirely up to the superintendent to what extent of doctoring that each one of them had. You had a camp doctor, was hired, which he was hired by the state, but he treated the convicts by call, like patients would go to him. We carried them to his office and he treated; his charges was according to what he did to them, but now if you had a convict, he came up to you and he said he had a fever or he had a pain in his back or his leg, if he had been there a little while you could tell whether he was putting the hat on you or not. But if he was new you had to do a lot of guessing, but now you had your own thermometer and you could pretty well tell when a person's sick. At night now, one of them got real bad-off sick at night and we carried him to the hospital; which what we'd do, we'd just carry him down there to the general hospital—the county hospital, whichever way you want to say it—and get him doctored on and the cost of it was just sent back to our camp doctor and he just put it on his bill; he would pay that. I don't know how but all the charges would be on his bill, which they had a form, a certain form that was printed in Montgomery; it would list his name, his serial number and the date, his diagnosis and what kind of medicine they give him, and the charges; and the doctor filled it out himself and it was notarized and the superintendent signed it once a month. They paid him once a month for what he did.

If you had an epidemic of something—I remember we was talking about pork and rice awhile ago—when I was at Grove Hill I had some convicts fix some pork and rice and—pork sausage and rice is what it was—and sent on the road and it made them all sick; they ate at twelve o'clock and at two o'clock we had about forty that I mean was really sick. Sick on the stomach, both ways. I mean they was so weak—and we called the doctor and he came and doctored on them, he stayed something like four hours 'till he got all of them straight. But that's the only time I remember the doctor having to come, you know, having to handle something at the camp.

Now, the superintendent ordered the medicine. It come from the central warehouse. You could get medicine that you couldn't buy in the drugstore, over the counter. The central warehouse was in Montgomery, which really it come out of the hospital up there. You ordered it from the state doctor, really, that was in charge of it. You ordered miazine drugs, penicillin, sulfa drugs—a fellow like me with a high-school education prescribing medicine! We used to use a lot of that kerosene and turpentine, too—for chest colds.

You ever heard of "many-weed tea"? I had a bunch one time in Grove Hill that had the flu, had about seven or eight that was sick. And I had a convict name of Matthew E. Anderson; he was raised in Thornton, he was about sixty years old, and he was a flunky inside the camp. Come up there one morning and he told me, "Captain Dees," he said, "if you'll let me make some many-weed tea," he says, "I'll cure them boys out there." And I said, "Well, Matthew E., I don't care, go ahead, but how you going to make it?" He said, "Well, you go out here in the pasture and pick up cow manure that's been there until it's dried and you boil that and put some lemon in it and a little vinegar." I said, "Oh, that won't cure a cold." He said, "Yes sir, Captain Dees, that'll cure it."

So he goes out there, I let him go, and he got it and wrapped it up in a sheet, put it on the fire and boiled it, put him some lemon in it, made him a tea, and them convicts drank four cups of it from time he made it to the next morning—and every one of them was a working the next morning! That's a fact. Now, I don't know if they knew what they were drinking. I never did tell them. I don't know if Matthew E. told them or not!

But what it did was made them—they all had fever and an hour after they drank it all of them was real wet with sweat. You've heard folks say if you go home and you take a toddy and put lemon in it and drink it and go to bed it will sweat your fever out, which I guess that reaction was the same. But it sure did put them on their feet. He also used to go get some other kind of root—I've forgotten what it was—he'd make a tea out of it, too.

He pulled a convict's tooth one day. He was old and he called all the convicts that was younger than him "sonny." And I had another one we called Moose Head—I forget what his name was. Reason we called him Moose Head, his head was all out of shape and he didn't have all that was coming to him. He had a tooth ache, up in the front, and he comes up there that morning and asked me would I carry him to the dentist, and I told him no I couldn't carry him that day 'cause the dentist's office was closed, he'd have to wait until the next day; and I give him some aspirin or something to kind of ease his pain off. That was about eight o'clock in the morning, there wasn't nobody there but me and the flunkies, everyone else had gone to work. This was when I was a steward at Grove Hill. And, well after awhile ol' Matthew come up there and asked me did I have any fishing cord, and I

told him yeah, there's some there in the desk. He got in the desk
and got it out, he started out the door, I was doing something,
something on the books; he started out and I said, "Matthew,
what you going to do with that?" He said, "Captain Dees, I'm
going to pull ol' Moose Head's tooth." I said, "Hell, you can't pull
that boy's tooth." He said, "Yeah, I can too, Captain." So, in a
little bit I got through what I was doing, walked back there, and
he had him laying down on the concrete sidewalk and he had tied
that string to his tooth and he wrapped that string around his
hand and he got it down about six inches from his mouth and he
actually put his foot on ol' Moose Head's head against that concrete and snatched that tooth out! He jumped up like he was
shot! But Matthew said he done it in the street when he was free.
He said he pulled everybody's tooth that would let him. He had
a remedy for every sickness. He'd fix you up.

It's funny about him. He was a minimum-custody prisoner
and he was first at Eight Mile. And they decided sometime back
then to make Eight Mile an all-white camp and—now wait a minute, they had had whites and they changed it to black and it was a
medium-custody camp and they was going to make it a minimum-
trusty camp—no guns. They had guarded them with guns. And
they had a big—William Carlson, he was in charge, worked with
the Board of Corrections—but anyway they had a big doing
down there that night—take the guns—and you know, they
talked to the convicts. He said any of you all who don't think they
can make it now without any guns over you, I want you to speak
up, and ol' Matthew E. raised his hand and he said go ahead, and
he knew him by name, said, "Go ahead Matthew E." He said,
"Captain Carlson, I could make it down here but I'm a long way
from home and I see the people from Grove Hill here; I sure
would like to go back with them, and be transferred to Camp
Grove Hill." And William Carlson turned around there and told
them to write his transfer out and let us carry him with us. That's
how we got about getting him. He was at Eight Mile.

They moved him to Grove Hill and he worked there in the
office, kept the office clean, what we call the front flunky that
done the office work and waited on the guards' table. He done
that for about a year, and we had to keep a man at the division
office to work up there and keep it clean around the office, and

the man up there went free and we sent him up there. And the day ol' Matthew went free them folks gave Matthew E. a party, the only convict I ever known to have a party when he left, and they gave him something like two hundred dollars. These were the personnel in the division office, your division engineers and the women that works in there, which there's about thirty or forty that worked in there. And they thought so much of ol' Matthew E. that they gave him a party whenever he went free, the day before he went free. Bought him a cake, bought him some clothes. He was just a typical southern nigger, if you want to put it that way. Now in the road camps they was supposed to be the best type of convict there was. Ordinarily he had to be. They had three classes: maximum security meant that he had to stay behind the walls; medium security meant that he could go to a road camp that had guns on a road guarding them; minimum security meant that he could go to an honor camp like we had at Eight Mile. He was a trusty. But now, let's say you didn't have no guns, that's the hardest kind to operate.

I done something one time that—Jennie Lee and I was talking one time about the percentage of people that had committed a crime that was under the influence of alcohol—one night I left here, it was something like eleven o'clock, and go down there and looked up all the files. I had looked up the type of crime and what the convict said himself—if he was drinking or under the influence of a kind of drug. It figured out, I think I had fifty-nine at the particular time, but anyway there was fifty-two of them was not himself when he committed the crime. Most all your murders that we get in the road camp are committed under the influence of alcohol. Or it's self-defense, or committed through fear. A black man, when he's scared, he'll hurt you. And then you got a type of black man here in the South is what they call a "bullie," and most of them that don't die of natural death, die, he's done scared another black man and he kills him.

Most violent fights I've seen in a road camp has been about homosexuals. Let me tell about an incident. It was in the evening when all the guards was there and it was—I didn't like to show no force around anybody because, if anybody'd see anything, there was nobody to testify against you if somebody was to push the fact that you did hit one of them. Anyway, as soon as everybody left I put a stop to that—quick. But I had been fishing over here, and I had got back and I carried the fish down there to get some of them to clean them for me, and Nichols, the bookkeeper then, he come out there where I was at. I asked him, I said, "Nichols, have you had any trouble?" "No, hadn't had a thing, everything's been mighty quiet Captain Dees," and about the time he got it out of his mouth "blam-de-bloom" inside the camp, and I looked at him and he looked at me, and I said, "What in the hell is that?"

And about that time this convict bailed out of the camp—his name was Stanley Dollard—and he was just bleeding all over. And a convict by the name of Davis had got on him with a meat cleaver, and he had cut his left arm off—the only thing that was holding it was the skin back there—and hit him in his cheek with it, hit him in his chest with it, on his arm two or three times, and the hand that he had cut off, he'd hit him twice.

I grabbed hold, and another convict was there, by the name of Charles Jackson, and I managed to artery his arm to keep it from bleeding so bad. I told Charles to hold it, and I run in there where the convict was and—you've heard the saying that a man was so mad that he stunk? Well, I actually smelled the fellow. His eyes was back in his head, and I asked him I said, "Give me that meat cleaver William," and he says, "Don't come no closer, Captain Dees," and it was a pick handle standing behind the door and I grabbed a hold of it. I said, "William, give me that meat cleaver," and he started backing up, and I said, "William, give me that meat cleaver," and all the time I was walking towards him, and he let me get in reach of him and when he did, he went one way and the meat cleaver went the other—that pick handle— but just the time I got him off the floor—I didn't hit him but one time—his eyes cleared up and he was just normal. But what had happened, he was trying—Dollard, the one he cut, was trying to make a gal boy out of him. He was fighting back, and he fought back, too.

The most blood I ever seen, though, was a boy by the name of Willie Jones was trying to do the same thing. This young boy— Jones pulled a knife on him one night; the next night Jones started fooling with him again and this boy had done, had an opportunity to get a hold of him a knife, and Jones pulled a knife back on him—and he just ought of not done it. That boy stuck him in the stomach and he stuck him in the liver; he cut him in the stomach three times, I believe. But anyway the little ol' convict, the orderly, Franklin, he was scared to death; young guy, good fellow, didn't cause any trouble, but before he realized what he was doing he was coming up the road there from the camp just screaming my name, "Captain Dees, Captain Dees, Captain Dees." Well, I jumped up went running down there, had another convict—name was Tommy Mills—was an orderly, Tommy was just mopping like heck. Ol' Jones was standing there, and they had just took just an armfull of towels and he was just holding them in his belly and blood just boiling out from under his arms. I told them to load him in the pickup. I never did think he would live, but he didn't die; we got him to the hospital in time.*

It sounds like we had a lot of that, but that's just two cases from '62 to '72. That's self-defense. That's not the only two fights I had with knives, but the rest of them was just little scratches. In ten years I had two cuttings over that, and actually, far as a man making a gal boy out of one in a road camp where the superintendent is strict, it's hardly ever heard of unless the superintendent went along with it because the other inmates looked down on it in a road camp. Bad. They would tell you what was going on, and if the superintendent had any sense of judgment at all he'll eliminate that. Just like these two cuttings; if it hadn't come so quick, if it had just waited two days before it boiled over, I would have known about it, but just like the day this fellow that done it, that cut the other one, he had been there two days and the one that cut Jones had been there three days. They had come from

---

*Jennie: "Pat, our oldest daughter, was outside with Fred when that prisoner came running up hollering so she ran outside and got the field glasses—we couldn't live without the field glasses! So she saw all this and gosh anytime anything like that happened it was several hours before we saw Fred. I thought I was going to have to take her to the doctor. She really got hysterical. She was in her teens then."

the medical center. But if it had been over a period of a week, if he could have put him off a week, the other inmates would have got to me and told me. Then I would have transferred him. I would have sent him back behind the walls. That's the quickest way to get your trouble ended, is to get the man that's trying to force it on one out of the way.

We let them have conjugal visits. Visitors, visitors. Female. It cuts your problems down, and the convict that has any respect for his family, he didn't want them to come in contact with no element like gal boys. So he would help you get rid of them.

But now, that was another rule that you bent. In other words, I done it in a way, I done it just like this: I said, "Now I'm not going to let no guard go to the wash house on visiting Sunday providing that if somebody comes checking they won't find nothing, and I won't know nothing, and if we get caught at it you can't say that I know." No guard knew.

For the single convict we had the loose girls that came. It gave them more to look forward to, in my opinion.

Let me give a good example of how I would do it. If I got a lot of trouble with whiskey inside the camp, all right let's get them all there and [say], "Let me tell you all, I can't let two things going on at one time; you all can either keep this damn whiskey out of this camp, or I'm going to lock the wash house door!" I *have* locked it up on visiting Sunday to show them that I would, and they would get a delegation back there to come to talk to me about it. And guess who would come? Their wives! And try to talk me into the notion of opening it up.

It puts his mind a little at ease about his life outside. But now every road camp didn't have that. You would take a road camp where the superintendent didn't have no feelings, well, you could tell, I could tell—I could get the escape reports each month and tell you quick which ones was doing it. Or I could get the classification records where they sent the convicts they have trouble with and send them back. You get a copy of all that was going on all over the state, where the convict was moving, and you could look at it, just like—let's use my camp and Grove Hill, for instance. I knew both them places was doing what I was doing,

ONE OF THE FEW STRUCTURES TO SURVIVE THE FIRE AT EIGHT MILE ROAD CAMP
WAS THIS BUILDING, REFERRED TO AS THE "WASH HOUSE," WHICH HOUSED THE CAMP
HOSPITAL (FAR END), THE LADIES RESTROOM, AND WASHING FACILITIES. A PORTION
OF THIS BUILDING WAS ALSO USED FOR CONJUGAL VISITS.

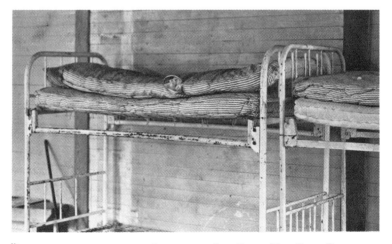

PART OF THE INTERIOR OF THE "WASH HOUSE" AT EIGHT MILE ROAD CAMP.

all right? But Camp Loxley wasn't, and actually that's what brought
the closing of Camp Loxley quicker than it did. Where we would
transfer maybe one man every two months, Loxley was transferring in two months fifteen and twenty. That's something to
wave at you, if you had a man and couldn't do nothing with him,
that was the way you got rid of him, or send him back into the
doghouse—solitary confinement—either one you want to call
it. And I never asked them to put but two men in solitary confinement—and I didn't ask them, I carried them up there and
demanded they put them in there. And I told them I didn't want
a transfer; I wanted him put in there fourteen days, and when
he comes out call me and I'll come and get him because I didn't
want the other inmates to think—say they get dissatisfied, maybe,
and say, "Well if I do a little something, Captain Dees will just
transfer me away from here." I didn't want him to use that for a
reason to get away from me.

You had to do it in a way so it doesn't come out, so it wouldn't
backfire in your face. That happened at one road camp. This
woman, from what I can tell happened, she'd been going with
different ones there, but she was going with this particular guy
and visiting him, and so one of the others that she had been visiting before, him and her got in an argument and he killed her;
he stuck a knife in her and cut her to death—inside the prison,
which caused a great big stink. And that happened, oh, that happened in '53 or '54, something like that. They let them go together, have sexual intercourse. They got inside a cell block like
the wash house at Eight Mile where the beds was and they would
put a blanket from the top bed down to the lower bed and it gave
them a little privacy—they called them "humps," is what they
called them, and it happened in one of them. And that stopped
all of that real quick. We got a letter as long as my arm the following week that said all visiting would be supervised direct.

It was general practice. They didn't have to be married, you
know. No way at all, no use to me lying, no. But, shoot, I let it go
on at Camp Eight Mile years after then. You can use it as a punishment stick, too. "I'm going to stop that if you all don't behave.
I'm going to stop that quick." And the inmates that wanted it bad,
they're the ones that wives come to see them regularly, they would
have a fit if you stopped it.

Well, the road camp looked like that—I'll draw a diagram.
Each one of these are trailers, they're ten-foot by forty-eight.
All the road camps looked the same. Now, they was put in and
these doors going place to place. They was ten trailers. Now, this
was the guards' sleeping quarters, this was the guards' dining
room, this was the kitchen. All right, we built a building in between—when we get down there to Eight Mile Camp you'll see
it—in between this trailer and this trailer, and made a dining
room out of it. This trailer here was the recreation hall, this was
a bath that we built 'cause the bath was so small, it had part of a
bath; and this was a bathroom we fixed; this was a cell, a cell, a
cell—had five cells. They slept in a cell that had room for the
beds, four double tiers, which slept sixteen men to the cell. So,
actually eighty men. Then, in back of the kitchen, was the supply
room, and in back of it the office. This is the office here. There
was a supply room; this was a steel door here that locked it off.
And we had a steel cage built here. This was a walk-in cooler at
this end of it. And this was a pass outdoors. In here was a steel
cage to where the kitchen had access to carry the garbage out,
and this end of the trailer was the guards' bathroom.

The trailers had a steel door at each end of it, and the windows
had steel bars over it, in other words, the windows were like this
and they took steel over the end of the wall and it was fastened
to it; it had bars cross it like that. ('Course, I still got one of the
trailers.) Now this was the wash house—the laundry, we call it the
wash house—and this was the hospital; this building is still down
here. This was a shack here, the only guard shack we had, and
the only time I put a man on it was on visiting Sunday, where he
could supervise the whole yard. That much of it was fenced in,
just a door here going outside. You lock this door, and the only
time we unlocked this door right here was to feed. As soon as they
got through eating, we locked it back, keep it all under lock and
key. But now, the fence, if one wanted to run, he could run anytime he wanted to; he could climb inside or outside the fence.

Down here was the actual camp location—I'll try and point it
out walking here. Over there, it held four beds, it slept the guards.
There's a wall in it right here, and then in through here was the

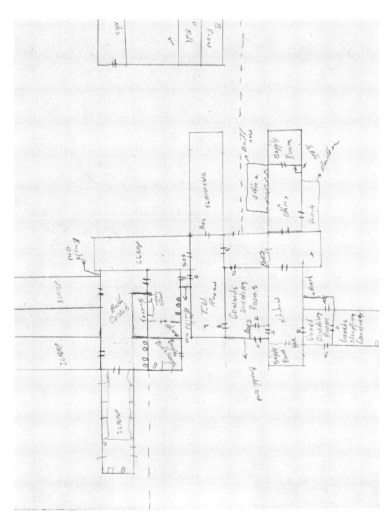

ROUGH DIAGRAM BY FRED DEES, SR.,
SHOWING THE APPROXIMATE LAYOUT OF EIGHT MILE.

guards' dining room, like on the diagram. That's the trailer that
was sticking out this way. Every trailer was that way, except the
building part that we built on to it. And when we get down here
you can see these, how we built onto it. They were all set up similar.
The trailer yonder? Was over yonder. You can see the old
foundation. All right, the kitchen—look on that paper. That
foundation there was the kitchen, that part is still there; the old
foundation is the dining room, the part that we built on, see.
Them bars yonder is this cage, here on the diagram. All right,
this trailer here, let's see the paper. This trailer here is this one
right here. This foundation right here. This foundation right
here is the one I marked "office."

All right, that foundation running yonder is one of the cells;
that one running yonder way is another cell. The entrance was
right here, that would have been the back of the trailer there.
This was the office to it; this was the front porch to it, and the
fence was right along here. That's the bathroom we built, and
that's the trailer that was a bathroom, and you've got your other
two going that way, your other three. And that's where the shack
was sitting. Those tables were part of the yard.

It's cool here, the trees do that. It was real pretty. We had the
yards full of flowers, shrubbery. It was one of the nicest yards,
locations, of the camps there was. The visitors sat out here and
inside too. The picnic tables are cement. We had tables all under
these trees, but we dug them up and put them out on the roads.
We had two tables under that tree, another one right in here,
and another one right across there. That fence, that's the property line, the fence went—see that concrete? That was a brace for
your post. There was one post there, and there was one post in
between out yonder. And the fence came in and went around
the shack and it went back out yonder to about that pile of dirt
and crossed back.

It operated until June of 1973. I came here in April of '62, then
I left the six months that I was off and I came back in June of '63
and been here ever since. The last camp I had was Eight Mile. It
was mixed at the time they closed, it burned a year after it was
closed, sat down there a year. Every trailer down there was built

on that style right there. They was all wooden buildings just like that. All of them had their humps in front where they could be moved around. Ball games, they'd get interested in a ball game, you could hear them laughing and carrying on and stuff. Noise, I never had no complaints from neighbors with noise.

It was a hot fire. They were 'tending to move these trailers and had a welder down here and burning on these pipes, and they figured they set it on fire accidentally.

What were the usual conditions that a prisoner would attempt to escape? When he was actually working on the road was when the majority would escape. He would catch the guard looking the other way and run, or either he would jump off the truck—which it was very easy for him to get away because he had all the opportunity in the world to get the drop on the guard. You very seldom lost them out of the camp. Once they got back to the camp they hardly ever run from the camp unless he was an orderly or a flunky that worked in the camp; then he would leave during the day when everybody else was out working.

Very few of the camps had dogs, but if you didn't have dogs you notified the Highway Patrol or the local sheriff enforcement. And the Board of Corrections had—like at Atmore they had a man that had dogs that you call, and they would bring them to you—which they used the dogs that way, and even if they didn't catch them right after you left, then you had to look for them.

For instance, the one run, say, when I was in Grove Hill. We would look for him sometimes three or four days, day and night. All the guards would look. What we would do, we would work the prisoners the regular hours, and we looked at night. It was hard thataway. Unless, sometimes you're lucky, he goes to a house or someone sees him and reports it to you. Pretty lucky. I would say you was real lucky to catch one right after he left. But the convict was—he didn't have any money or anything and he had to contact his people. And they staked out his house and such as that. I've caught several as he got home, when he got home.

We had a house staked out at Frisco City one time. Buddy of mine, it was on Christmas Day, and the man who had it was there, and he called us, the superintendent and I, and told us the man was in the house. So we drove to the house and the superintendent tells me to go to the back door and he was going to the front door. When he knocked on the door and hollered who he was— Richard English was exactly his name—"Richard, come on out of there, we know you're in there." Instead of Richard coming out, he made a beeline for the back door and the house was sitting something like six foot off the ground in the back of it, and I had stepped up on about the second door step and was standing there and when I heard him running, I had a pistol in my hand, and when he come out of that door, he just jumped out the back door, and when he did, he jumped on me—and that knocked me— and landed on top of me and in the process the gun went off—I pulled the trigger on the gun. And when we hit the ground, like I said, Richard was on top of me and I pushed him off and finally got around and got my flashlight—he knocked my flashlight out of my hand, too—and when I shined the light on him he was bleeding in the head and it just scared the devil out of me. I thought I had shot him, but I could see that he was breathing, so I touched him on the foot and said, "Richard get up from there." And he just jumped right straight up. But the bullet did hit him, the bullet grazed him across the head.

He was the worst beat-up convict after an escape I ever seen. We started back to Grove Hill with him and the superintendent, he stopped and got him a limb and he beat him—now, he really beat him. When we got back to Grove Hill he had done bled a big place in the back of the truck and I asked the superintendent if he wanted to carry him to the doctor. At first he told me, "No, hell no, I ain't carrying the son of a bitch to the doctor." Then I told him, "You'd better do something for him." He told me to stop—I was driving—and he got the light and looked at him, and he said, "Yeah, I guess we had." So we carried him to the doctor. He was the worst, bloodiest convict for signs. You could see the signs on him where he had been beaten. I believe he was in for grand larceny. The reason he escaped, which could be seen through very easily, his wife was pregnant when he got in, and she had the baby and wrote a letter stating she was real sick and didn't know if the baby was going to live or not; so he went

Fred Dees, Sr., approaching the site of burned-out Eight Mile Road Camp.

Picnic grounds and a guardhouse seen through barred windows at Loxley Road Camp.

GUARD SHACK AND A PORTION OF THE PICNIC AREA AT LOXLEY ROAD CAMP.

home to see about her. But the reason that he was beat so bad, I guess, the reason the superintendent let his temper get away with him, was because he run the day before Christmas Eve and by him doing that caused all of us to have to work day and night through Christmas. Ordinarily, we would have been at home. I didn't feel that guilty; it made me feel bad, too, 'cause I had to work on Christmas.

When I came to Eight Mile, if I had one lost, all I did was report him. The only way I would go look for one was for someone to call me and say they had just seen him and he wasn't moving. What I mean by that he was in a house somewhere and I would go look for him, but I didn't really like to. I got to feeling that's what they paid the law for; they didn't pay me to get escaped convicts.

But now, at Grove Hill it sounds like we lost a lot of convicts, but we went there one time four years at Grove Hill and nobody run. That's right, and in the first seven years that I run the camp at Eight Mile I lost four convicts in seven years.

I think the difference is the treatment and the food. The food plays a big part of it, and maybe it's letting them know that you care about their problems. I feel like that did more good than anything. When a man escaped it hurt everybody. Everybody felt the effects of it because the guards and the superintendent would get mad and they would be hard to get along with and by having to work day and night, and naturally the convicts felt it.

I'm sure there was times when a convict would talk another out of running. I don't know the number or instances right offhand, but I'm sure. Which, now at Eight Mile I was told one morning after it was integrated—we had whites—one of the blacks told me that one of the whites had put on his Sunday clothes, they called it, the clothes they kept real clean and fixed for visiting. He had his white clothes underneath his work clothes, and that morning when I checked out I just held him out. But all I did was postpone it; he just didn't run that day, he run something like a month after that.

Usually, they came to the road camp after going to prison. But we got a lot of them right off the streets because of the crime they committed and their record in the streets would determine, would tell them a lot, which they made a lot of mistakes; most of the convicts you lost within three days after they got there. But the men that classified them, that determined where to send them, whether they would stay behind the walls or be put on the farm or sent to a road camp, I feel like they did an excellent job, because they could screen men day in and day out and just move very few of them. They've done a good job of doing that, I'll have to say that; they've done an excellent job. A lot of first offenders went to road camps if he had any age on him, but a young man, if he was a first offender and young, he automatically went to Draper. Because they tried to at Draper—it was the first prison in Alabama set up for rehabilitation, it was strictly for that even way back, oh fifteen years ago. A man could go to school there and finish high school.

We had lots of situations and different kinds of convicts. For instance, we had one convict, he parched peanuts. He worked at the division office and he parched peanuts every day and brought them back to the office. This particular evening—he always parched them in a big pan and then he always sacked them up when he got back to the camp—he come walking in, he always got in before the convicts on the road did. He was real goosy; you could walk up behind him and touch him on his side or on his head or most anywhere and he would say what was on his mind—what he was thinking about to himself. And this particular evening Charles Milburn, which he was over the bureau of maintenance for the state, and Mr. Shaw, which was over the convict operation for the Highway Department, and two, three more sitting there—I don't remember exactly who all, but the office was full of people. And "Texas," that's what we called the convict, was real particular about his manners and everything, and when he come in there he'd say, "Checking in, Captain Dees." I'd say "Okay, Texas." He had a big thing of peanuts and ol' Charles Milburn was a big eater and he asked him, said, "Boy what you got there?" Ol' Texas, "Got some peanuts, Captain, would you care for some?" He was passing them around and when he got to Charles Milburn I just touched Texas with my foot and he just poured the peanuts over Charles Milburn and said, "Take all the goddamn peanuts you want to!"

Another time these two convicts escaped, which this was in the north end of our district, which was up around Pine Hill. At the time, I worked at Grove Hill. We had put the dogs on them early in the morning, and we had run them coming back south right along the railroad track all day and we lost track about dusk, dark. So, we all went in at night, but the superintendent just insisted that I stay at the railroad depot at Whatley. I told him all right. About three o'clock in the morning I was sitting up there on the porch of the depot and it was just black dark, and I could hear somebody walking down the railroad track. At night you can hear somebody on that slag along that a long ways off, and I got to listening, reckon it got a little closer. In a few minutes I could hear talking to one another. Both of them was brave, you know. One of them asked the other, "What would you do if Captain Dees just stepped right out here?" The other said, "I'd just knock him down." And the other said, "You know what I'd do, I'd just jump on him here and just stomp him to death." They walked on up there and when they got there where it was no way to get away, I said, "Now where in the world are you two boys going?" The other said, "I told you to quit talking about Captain Dees!"

Now, another was Willie Watson. He was a trusty. So, we sent Willie to Eight Mile from Grove Hill. I got transferred from Grove Hill to Eight Mile and I had Willie again. So, Willie he wrote up several writs for one thing or another, I never. And he got so bad that any time I would punish a convict, he would be his lawyer. It got to whenever I had to punish one, I'd just call Willie up there and just let him defend him. Weren't no hard feelings, me and Willie was good friends, but I would call him up there and say one of them got drunk or broke something or one of my rules. I would call the convict up there and then holler back there for Willie Watson to come up there and I'd tell Willie to defend him. And I said, "If you need any time with your client, just go back there and talk to him, and when you-all get ready to defend you-all's case, you-all just bring it on up here." So he'd talk for him; the convict didn't have a bit of sense, he was guilty when he let Willie handle his case, but he thought he was being— but anyway, Willie, he was a wash-house convict, in other words he was the convict that run the wash house, washing all the convicts' clothes. One day he told me that he wanted to talk to me, and I told him all right. He said, "Seriously, Captain Dees, I really want to talk to you, I found out something I want to talk to you about, but," he said, "I don't want to talk to you in front of nobody."

So that night after I ate supper I told Jennie Lee I was going to walk back down to camp. I went down there to the wash house where Willie was by himself and I told Willie, I said, "Okay, Willie, what do you have to say?" "Captain Dees, you know I got this thing figured out." I said, "How's that Willie," and he said, "If I run and can get in a state—it don't make too much difference which state it is—and get caught and fight extradition on the ground that I've been convicted illegally, I could beat my case." I said, "Oh, Willie you can't do that." He said, "Yes sir, I can too." So, he got his law book out and I just sat and listened to him and just talked to him like really talking. Now, I told him if he thought that was what to do, that'd be the best thing to do!

About a week after this, one night he come up there and told the guard that he had some ironing to do down at the wash house, (they were letting him go and come); about two o'clock they called me and said Willie Watson done gone—his nickname was "Cream"—that Cream had gone. The reason they called him Cream was 'cause he was so dark, we had to give him a name that would lighten him up a bit. But anyway, so he did that, he went to a state—I think he went to Illinois or somewhere—he turned himself in and sure enough he beat it. But he died about six months after he got out of the penitentiary. They found him dead in a boardinghouse.

I had another that was gone three years. Then one day a woman came to the door and she asked if Captain Dees here and I said yeah and she said, "Well, Captain Dees, I got Leroy out there in the car. I told you if I ever found him I would bring him back to you." So, I hollered out there and told ol' Leroy to come in. Three years, he'd been gone three years. I asked him what he'd been doing and he told me. I asked him what made him decide to come back and he told me he just got tired of darting. "I just got tired of darting," he said. "I'm ready to try to make amends for what I done. I just hopes that they'll let me stay down here with you." I guess he stayed up here in the house, and then I carried him back down there and put him in convict clothes. But he couldn't stay there. After an escapee stays out a year he has to go back to the medical center to be examined, and they reclassified him and the board decided maybe they should let him go to Atmore. I've heard from him—he's out now—but I haven't seen him. One day I'll see him on the streets of Mobile.

They first started to integrate in '69, '69, or '70, I think. The cells were mixed. They slept in the same cell. When they first, I had fifty-two blacks, and they sent me eight whites. I had five cells and I put one in each cell and then two to make it, but I had a white in each cell; it was integrated. It didn't help the convict, black or white; they was already living under the same conditions, both of them was. The only thing that they separated, the white was living on one side of the penitentiary and the black was living on the other side of it. That was in the penitentiary, not the road camps.

They all ate out of the same pot. They didn't have plates for a white man and plates for a black. They went to the picture show together. They didn't say whites sit here and colored over here. When they went to the picture show—the reason I know is 'cause I used to go in with them—they'd mix up. This was all in the regular penitentiaries. The big deal that the paper played up on segregation in the penitentiary was just a cahoot, anyway. The only thing that really changed was the road camps. They had black and white road camps and they mixed them up; that's about the only thing that changed. They used the same toilets. And when, like on Saturday and Sunday, they was turned out in the yard together, they associated with one another before the integration thing come.

A penitentiary is a bad place to start integration 'cause they lived under the same warden, the same rules and everything.

The only problem it caused was the guards. The guards wanted to show partiality toward the whites, and the blacks wanted the

same opportunity as the whites, which I don't blame them for.
If a guard showed him partiality, maybe he was supposed to come
out here to bring him something, say he was white, the convict
asked the guard to let him speak to him and he did, and then
maybe fifteen minutes later here come a black family and the
black man asked the guard, "Can I do so-and-so?" What you're
doing is against the rules, and that's the worst problem it caused
me, 'cause I have to stress to the guard that he's creating a bad
problem, and finally I got it across to them about after a year.

The blacks, they brought that to me; I was the only one that had
the authority to straighten it up, so instead of arguing amongst
themselves they brought it to me. Everytime I called them together as a group to talk to them I stressed in their mind that
problem. I was the only one that could straighten them out, and
as long as I could keep it in their mind they would bring them
to me.

I had one boy, for instance, that was going up for parole. He
had been here four or five years; he was a "flunky." We call a
flunky a man who works inside a prison, he stays here all the time.
What he does is clean up after everybody who's going to work and
during the day his job is to keep the yard clean, clean the camp.
He's called a flunky. I mentioned that before. And, ah, Leroy, I
spoke about him before, too, was going up for parole. And I was
gone on the Saturday he got his letter that they turned him down,
and he didn't have nobody to talk to. I felt like if I had a been
here, I never would have given the letter to him; I could have
talked to him. But the man I had left in charge, he had no feelings
for nobody, and he just throwed the letter on him, and when he
did, it shocked Leroy so bad that he run.

Now, the discipline has changed, too. When Daddy started
he handled convicts strictly from fear. Even in the field, a man
was out there won't—say they was chopping cotton and he was
behind them, way behind the rest of them—they didn't try no
reasoning with him. They laid him down right there and whupped
him and put him right back there and made him do it. But when
I started in '52 they had done away with the strap (like Daddy
was talking). But we had the hose type, and then it come along,
when I was tried in court, everybody got scared to use force and

then things really changed; then that you started—let me tell you—you started using, putting the hat on the convict, really. You would listen to him a certain extent; then you would figure out what to say to him to make him do like you wanted him to. And then, but you had some that you couldn't, he wouldn't listen to you for twenty-four hours. One convict I had was named Billie Thomas. I couldn't do nothing with him, but you take Little Fred, he got him to do like he was supposed to when he was doing summer work at Eight Mile. While he was on furlough he come to see Little Fred, but he didn't come to see me because I never could do nothing with him. But he came from a real good family. Now, his daddy and mother, his sisters and brothers, they was educated and they was in high society in Mobile, but they couldn't figure out what was wrong with Billie.

Once I had a convict named Larry Lee Smith, happiest man I have ever dealt with in the penitentiary, and one of the meanest men I ever dealt with. He had been to several road camps; fact of the matter he had twenty-five years, and then when he was at Chatham he forged a check on a guard up there and got two more years. Then they sent him down to me, and Larry Lee would do just most anything it struck him to do, and I had done about decided that I was going to have to send him back.

I called him this evening. He was working with a mechanic, and the mechanic was really a sorry man, and he had carried Larry Lee off that evening, and got off at home and told Larry Lee to bring the truck back here. Well, I waited and waited and waited and he didn't come. Now he lived at Chunchula and I went up there and I found Larry Lee—well, I found the truck parked on the side of the road, and I just waited. Sure enough, here come Larry Lee. I told him to just get on the back of the pickup and I drove on to see a man that had called about a drive-way, and when I got back in the truck and started off.

Larry Lee says, "Captain Dees," he says, "I know I done wrong, and I know that you fixing to send me away." "But," he said, "If you'll do me like my daddy used to," he said, "I'd appreciate it." I knew what he was talking about, but I'm going to make him tell me. I said, "What you want Larry Lee?" He said, "Captain Dees, just carry me out here in these woods and give me a good spanking, and then let's you and me go back to the camp and I won't do it no more." Well, I took him at his word and I spanked him, and then he changed. He called me Daddy from that day.

On the day he got out—I helped him get out on parole and it was hard to get him out—it wasn't just a little while after he got out he started working driving a truck and him and his brother bought their own truck together, and they was making good money. But anyway, his mother passed away, and within forty-five minutes from the time he found that out he was sitting out here in front of the house to come tell me his mother died. And he stayed here for something like three hours. But he called me Daddy. Everytime I see him now, he calls me Daddy. But cases like that I like to remember because I think I helped him.

Little Fred will tell you this, the handling of them. Some you come attached to, real attached to, some you dread to see. And it's just personality, really—his attitude and his personality. I think his attitude has more to do with it.

Now, the convicts try the same thing. They try to figure you out, too. Actually, they figure that anyone at all with any ambition won't be working at a convict camp. They figure that a guard, foreman, or whoever he might be, can't work nowhere else. And it would be easy for a person to be real bitter if he let that touch him.

There was this road camp and it had a population of over one hundred men, and they was having just worlds and worlds of trouble with them; and they transferred me down there to try to straighten it out. Well, the guards down there resented it 'cause, actually, I was young. I was; when I started off I wasn't but twenty-two years old. I was the youngest steward they ever had, and when I made superintendent I was the youngest superintendent they've ever had to run a convict camp. But anyway, it wasn't but the fourth, fifth night I was down there that two of the convicts started fighting in the recreation hall with knives. Both had knives, and all together I would imagine it was ten—between

ten and fifteen—guards there, the ones on duty and then the
ones that was boarding, and the man that was on duty in the
recreation hall came out and locked the door behind him.

Well, I run back in and told him to open the door. Where I
had been working it had always been that when you went in a
situation like this, they backed you up. Well, I just went straight
into the two convicts that was fighting and pulled them apart.
The next thing I noticed was that the convicts just come around
me, in a small circle. And to get out of situations like that you
act like a crazy man; you do it quick—just scream, holler, cuss,
hit everything that's in reach, see—and when I did that they
just backed up.

The shock of something like that just scared the hell out of
you, and this time they moved back, I knew they wouldn't fight
no more so I made for the door, and they had to unlock the door
to let me out! They locked me in, and all the guards standing outside looking in. They wanted it to happen 'cause I was a stranger
there. The word was sent out that I was coming down there to
straighten it out. They do you that way.

But over a period of '62 to '72, when they closed the camp,
the only time that I used—I never took one of them out there
and got his attention—the only time that I used force any way,
was when they was fighting amongst themselves. To separate
them, I used that as an excuse to get my lick or two in, and on
several occasions, if I had two who couldn't get along, that just
kept fighting, I would just make them fight—make them fight
'til they'd get so tired they could hardly move and then I would
make them kiss one another, hug one another, and nine times
out of ten they become best friends. I just let them work it out of
their systems, which it was strictly against the rules, but rules
was made to bend anyway.

In a penitentiary now, like me, the guards hardly ever got
transferred from one camp to another, but like when I was working at Grove Hill and got transferred to Loxley, they tried me,
them convicts had heard about me. They said, "Well, let's test
him out." And it didn't take but five or six slaps and two or three
kicks and a lot of loud talk and cussing and it was all over with.
They quit it quick.

They could buy knives; in the road camp they could buy knives. They had weapons, but I never got scratched.

Another time we had a houseboy that worked in the house every day. And I had pretty close to two hundred dollars of old coins and they disappeared; actually they disappeared the first weekend that we stayed over in our new fishing cabin. And I was just raising hell, and I was telling Jennie what I was going to do to ol' John Hamilton, that was the convict's name. He was the only one who had access to the house. But she told me that I shouldn't talk like that and I told her if she'd run that up there, I'd run that down yonder. She told me I ought to be ashamed. At that particular time, if I had gone down there me and John Hamilton would have gone round and round, but I didn't get my money, I never did find it. Two hundred dollars in old coins, silver coins, too. But, you lose a lot of stuff. How did I confront him? With a hickory stick. He denied it. I didn't get it out of him, but I didn't really try too hard.

I didn't act hastily, I—a lot of the old foremans that worked under me said I was too easy on convicts, which you turn it right around, the convicts would take it that I was strict. The guards that said that, they never seen me hit one, but then the convict knew that I *would*. That was the difference. I didn't try to sell the fact that I would hit one.

Since they've closed that camp down yonder at Eight Mile— about a month before they closed that camp down there I got the letter telling it, but they closed it before it came in effect— the new rules on discipline. If a man, a convict, broke one of the rules—I'm going to say for drinking, let's say for being drunk— say a guard caught him on the road with whiskey, he brought him in the prison and you sat down and made out a report on it, and he signed it. And you gave him a copy of it and you set a day, right then, for him to be tried for that offense. And then he can make his preparation to plead—for him to show that he was not guilty. And the guard sat on one side and the convict sat on the other, if the guard said something about it the convict didn't like, the convict now had the authority to tell the guard he's a damn liar. It's a mess now.

Now, the doghouse was another way of punishing the convict back then. It was a room, it was just a bunch of rooms built in a horseshoe shape. It had a steel door that was sealed; when it closed, you couldn't see your hand in front of you. It had a drain in the middle of it, but they give them a bucket to go to the bathroom in. And they took it out once a day, every twenty-four hours. You had to feel for it. And they would put as many as eight men in that five-by-eight room. This was a hole, the doghouse. A lot of folks called it the hole and a lot of people called it the doghouse. And they'd put him in there for twenty-one days and they would feed him one time a day.

In the doghouse they fed him one time a day—and that was a piece of corn bread and a glass of water. Every third day they gave him one meal, a balanced meal. Just one meal. They were put in there without any clothes. He would lose—I've seen them put in there, I've *carried* a man and put him in it, and he'd say, weigh one hundred eighty pounds, and when I'd get him back after twenty-one days he'd weigh less than one hundred twenty. And that's not good for you. You're starving him to death is what you're doing.*

They put a fellow by the name of Robert Andrews in there. He ran the prison at Kilby, he was the only white convict there, which he was accused, which he said he didn't do it, of killing a FBI agent and stealing his car. He had a life sentence and he got out on parole, which Daddy helped him get out. Then he got back in. He led an escape out of Draper. They put him in there and told him they was going to put him in there until he asked to get out. And they toted him out on a stretcher. He never asked to get out; he was that kind of man.

Very few camps had a doghouse. I never worked at a camp that had one. We took ours to Atmore. At Grove Hill sometimes we carried them to Montgomery, but most of the time we brought them to Atmore. But now, when I was at Eight Mile I brought all of mine to Atmore. It wasn't too often, maybe twice a year,

---

*Oscar Dees: "They got where now they give them a meal every day, which is not no punishment to it now, at all."

something like that. All the problems you could solve yourself—
if you could solve yourself—you would not have as many, but if
you started hauling them away from there, it seemed to me like
the more you did it, the more you had to do it. So you tried to
solve all that, as much of it as you could, without doing that.

Today they've changed all that. They've lit them up now, and
they've got a commode in all of them. That's something else that
the public—the federal government, whenever all this segregation mess and civil-rights things was coming out—they done
away, that's another thing they done away with.

I've tried to control convicts on the basis that let me reason
with you, but now if you won't reason with me—I'll treat you
like a human being, like a man. I didn't only try to sell an idea; I
told them face to face, "I'll treat you like a man as long as you'll
treat me as one." And along with that you have to put, you have
to let them know that if they don't do that, that you'll do something. It's not all bullshit, is my words, it's not all bullshit that
you're trying to sell them. But you have to let them know that
you're not playing.

Oh, I have thrown fits down there amongst those men, pulled
my shirt off, kicked my shoes off, thrown my glasses down, acting
like somebody crazy, just begging one of them to jump on me.
You have to do that, you have to put up a certain amount of front.
But now, he's smart—don't sell him short; don't sell the convict
short, because he knows when to say, he knows when to bring
you a cup of coffee and keep his mouth shut. He knows when to
bring you a cup of coffee with a smile. Now you take the men
that could see me in the morning, I could come out of the house,
and I always walked down the middle of the road to the camp,
and they all watched me; they could tell by the way I walked what
kind of mood I was in. A black man, he's studied psychology
anyway. 'Cause that's who should be teaching psychology in all
your colleges. 'Cause *he* knows. Just talk to him from the time he
was a child to [when] he gets grown.

Which, I feel like my daddy—I got a great feeling of being—
things said about him in the respect Captain Dees would kick
your butt, or he would knock you down. I wanted the convict to

say, "Captain Dees would treat me fair." More so that I would personally. I just don't know how Daddy's feelings in it was. I have questioned several guards and informers I worked; I never could get no sense really out of them. But when I punish my own kids with a switch, I worry about it. And I done the same thing when I punished the convicts. And I have talked to several, like I said, guards, then I have talked to several—well, William Carlson for one. He beat convicts half to death all his time he was in the penal system—he told me I was soft. And the superintendent that I started under, he had no feelings for convicts.

The most mad you get though is, to take one—well, I had a convict named Tommy—I called his name awhile ago, he came from Tuscaloosa—and Tommy was, I guess you could call, a good man in the streets. What he did, Tommy had a good job, making good money, and two or three of the men that he run around with—and he was younger—got to picking at him, running over him. Well, Tommy got to feeling that they was going to whup him. So one day they told him that when you get paid Friday we're going to take your money. Tommy went right straight then to the pawnshop and bought him a pistol. And he killed one of them and shot the other two that Friday night. No questions asked! He just went to the beer joint where they was at and called them out. He got ten years, I think, for it, or maybe fifteen years, and they sent him to the camp. Well, escape was wrote all over his face. I took a lot of patience with him, I mean a lot of patience, and I talked him out of that escape, which after three days he finally told me that he was going to escape. And I called his momma in Tuscaloosa and talked to her, and I told her if it was anyway possible for her to come—the following Sunday was visiting Sunday—and told her if it was any way possible to bring his wife and two kids too with her, which she did. Well, Tommy never worked a day on the road. I made him the office flunky, and Nichols was the bookkeeper, and he had the best personality of anybody I worked around in a convict camp and ol' Tommy just fell in love with Nichols.

In about a year and I got wind that Tommy was bootlegging whiskey in the camp. The man that lives right behind Eight Mile is a moonshiner, and Tommy has got him up a deal; he was buying whiskey from that man and reselling it in the camp. So, one Sunday I set up to catch him and I did catch him. And it hurt me to think I had took all that time and then he let me down; I didn't let him down, he let me down. When I did start questioning him about it, Tommy made the mistake of telling me a lie, and I really lost my temper and I really flew into him, with not no stick or nothing, in other words just like if you and me got to arguing. I was ready to fight and I fought and begged him to fight back, but in thirty minutes after it was over with he come up there and apologized, shook my hand and promised me it would never happen again. And it didn't, which he's out today. On parole back in Tuscaloosa. But when you put a lot of time in one and he lets you down, it makes you fighting mad. And they will let you down. They'll do that.

I mentioned the trial before. Another fellow and me was charged with whupping a convict. Well, that's not exactly the way. Anyway, it happened in February of 1961. At Grove Hill.

The convict worked in the division office, that's the main office; he was the orderly up there, cleaning up and everything. He was in for grand larceny. He was what your colored people would call today an Uncle Tom, just a regular plaything. He could dance, he was small, and he dressed—kept his white convict clothes starched and ironed, and he worked in that office around the big shots. Everybody thought a lot of him, and, see, he got off at five, and we didn't check in 'til six in the evening, and he'd go back there and eat his supper and then, just take the time— Jennie Lee was living at Atmore and I was boarding there at the prison, and I had a private room and all, right there at the convict camp, and 'stead of staying back there with the rest of the convicts, Hucklebuck, that's what we called him, would come up to the office where I was at, sit around there and read the paper, which he was a trusty and everything, you know.

I'd get up about bedtime and he'd say, "Captain Dees, you going to take a bath now?" And I'd say, "Yeah," and he'd go back there and lay me a towel out and lay my clothes out, and I'd take a bath and crawl up in the bed and he'd shave me. Shave me every night for about two years that I was there. He'd stay around me 'til about nine o'clock every night, and it just happened that he just got caught in the circumstances.

They had a cabinet there at the office that held certain records in it, stamps and all. They called it a safe, but actually it was just a little ol' metal box, didn't even have a lock on it. And he was suspected of taking it.

When the cabinet come up missing, they called Mr. Moore, he was the division engineer, and told him someone had broke into the division office. And they had an investigation. And this happened on Sunday. I was at home, we were living at Atmore weekends. So, I go back up there on a Monday and they were holding a big investigation up there at the office. And they brought the little ol' convict down there that evening. Mr. Gibson, he was the superintendent or warden, whatever you want to call him; I was the bookkeeper. And he told me to feed him and lock him up—that he was going to carry him back to the office. So I did, and then he came back about nine o'clock that night and told me that the little ol' convict had got sassy right there in the office.

But he didn't confess. He confessed later on to Daddy, and we had to transfer him. Daddy was working at Atmore prison at that time and we brought him down there, and Daddy talked to him one day and he told Daddy all about it.

Later, an affidavit was signed by Hucklebuck stating that me and Mr. Gibson whupped him trying to make him confess to breaking in and stealing that cabinet. They carried it before the grand jury, got it indicted. On the grounds that we whupped this convict to make him confess to a crime he didn't commit.

It was filed with the FBI office in Mobile, and the FBI office sent agents. They come, and they got two statements from me before I was indicted. And then they done the investigation and they carried the convict and some others down there before the grand jury of eighteen men. And Hucklebuck told them his side of it, and they indicted us on his say-so.

They not only tried to indict us, they tried to indict the sheriff up there, of Clark County, and Mr. Moore, he was the division engineer, they tried to indict him, and the fellow by the name of Samuel Coleman, he was an investigator with the Highway Patrol, Department of Safety, that was called there to investigate it.

They tried to say—well, they did say—those three whupped the
convict in the office and tried to make him say that, and then
he was brought down to the convict camp where I was at and
then me and Mr. Gibson whupped him down there trying to
make him say it. But now, when it got before the grand jury, they
just had enough evidence to try me and Mr. Gibson, they figured.
I thought as much of Mr. Gibson as I did of my father; fact of
the matter, I think I would have done more for him than I would
have for my father. But when it got to court he got up there and
testified that he brought the convict and left him with me, and
went back to the office. And the deputy sheriff and the division
engineer also testified that he wasn't gone but ten minutes. That
was in the trial.

The charge had something to do with force, it wasn't civil
rights, it forced—violated the convict's rights by use of force,
something like that.*

Then I got indicted. Surprised? No. I figured it was coming
all along. Then they put it on the radio, that's the funny part:
they printed it in the paper that day that the FBI was looking for
me like I was running!

Even when they indicted me, a couple of weeks after then I
got to thinking how bad I had been mistreated. I felt I had been
mistreated, and by me drinking and thinking about it so strong
that I could have killed them that was responsible for it—easy.
You feel frustrated and you want to fight back. That's the only
thing you can think about—is getting even.

And another thing, the time that all this happened there was
a lot of people being transferred all over the state; it was a mess.
Everybody was running around telling them this and that and
they was transferring folks. Just stirring up a darn mess.

---

*Criminal Case No. 14,263 in the United States District Court for the
Southern District of Alabama. The formal complaint was 'unlawful
assault upon a prisoner for the purpose of inflicting summary punishment upon him and/or coercing an admission or confession in depriva-
tion of his right and privilege not to be deprived of liberty without due
process of law or to be subjected to punishment without due process
of law, all in violation of Section 242 of Title 18, United States Code'—
David R. Coley, III, Coley & Coley, Mobile, Alabama, defense attorneys.

But that's how come during this time, before they laid me off, well, they transferred me away from Grove Hill to Eight Mile, and then I went down there and I was bookkeeper and then I became warden down there; they didn't go along with that, so they transferred me again to North Alabama—Russellville—and I stayed in North Alabama two or three months. That was in the First Division. I had to report to Decatur when I left Eight Mile.

I worked in Eight Mile ten months before I was tried and they decided they'd better send me a little further away from home, I guess. During those ten months was when the FBI came to me twice and asked for a statement. They was investigating it during those ten months.

Really and truly, if you want to know the truth, they tried to make me quit. Thats's the whole thing in a nutshell. They wanted me to quit—this was during the time they was trying to get an indictment against me and Mr. Gibson. And they were trying to make it as hard on me as they could. They sent me up there. Also, I reported to Decatur, which is the division office, and then they sent me to Russellville. It was a convict camp. The superintendent there was a good friend of my daddy's, been knowing Daddy and been knowing me a long time. And he told me after I went to work there—I hadn't been there two, three days—he told me he had orders to try to make me quit. Fact of the matter he told me that they told him not to let me off but two days at a time. By doing that I wouldn't be able to come home. It took me five hours and thirty minutes to drive it from there to Atmore— one way. I was right on the Tennessee line.

Well, I stayed there from February until April 1962, until the suspension. After the suspension I was on leave without pay. From April to October, 1962. They wrote me a letter then—I got something like three days after I was arrested—that I had been suspended for thirty days and at the end of that thirty days, if I hadn't been cleared of this charge, I would be automatically fired; which there was no way in the world for me to get out of it in thirty days. Also, the rules and regulations said that if you get suspended thirty days within a twelve month period that you can be fired. So, that's what they used, they suspended me thirty days and at the end of that thirty days they was planning on firing me. We made an appointment to see the highway director. The

Highway Department has got a director which is appointed by
your governor, and he's boss over all the operations of the Highway Department, except the personnel office is not under him.
But we went up there to talk to him and he wouldn't talk to us.
Later, I don't remember what day it was, me and Mr. Gibson
went to Montgomery and talked to the personnel board. And
the man in charge of the personnel board, name was Hooper, and
while we was in his office he called the highway director, called
him and told him that he was going to have to change that letter
because we had not been found guilty of any charges, that the
only thing he could do with us is to put us on leave without pay
until we were proven innocent or guilty. And if we was found
innocent, he would automatically have to put us back to work.

When they arrested me is when they suspended me. At first
now, let me straighten this out. The first letter that I got from the
personnel board, they fired me. I got that letter after I come
home and I left up there the 15th of April, so I must have got it
somewhere between the 15th and the 20th. After I had been
arrested. I don't remember exactly; the warrant had been issued
for me before the 15th of April and the 15th of April was on a
Saturday, I believe it was, but Mr. Gibson called me on a Friday
from Grove Hill and told me he had been arrested. I was at Russellville, working. And he told me that they had already arrested
him. He had to make bond. And then Daddy called me just a
little short time after then, something like thirty minutes after Mr.
Gibson did, told me to get in that damn car and come home because, he said, they had sent the warrant for me to Florence,
Alabama, which is, I guess, the closest place they had a office. He
told me if they arrested me up there that somebody from here,
by nobody knowing me up there, would have to drive up there
and then get somebody up there to make bond for me before I
could get out.*

---

*Jennie: "The first I knew about it was Fred's daddy called me to tell
me that Fred had been indicted, and that was before Fred even knew
it, and I was just wondering how he knew; I never thought to ask how
he knew that."

So, I came home to Atmore, and that Monday evening I called Cunningham. He was the federal marshal; his daddy used to be a judge down here at Bay Minette. I knew Cunningham and played football against him. The radio and everything, they was still looking for that fugitive, Fred Dees—he had run off; this was in the papers, too. Anyway, that evening I went up to a lawyer I knew at Atmore and told him what I was up against, and he asked me did I know Howard Cunningham, the federal marshal, and I told him I did. He said, "I'll tell you what we'll do, Fred, we'll just call him." So he called him for me and I talked to him after he got on the phone, and he told me to be down in Mobile the next morning at nine o'clock and be sitting in the hall when he got to work. And told me to bring somebody to go my bond. While they was fingerprinting me and all of that jive, which took something like twenty minutes, Howard Cunningham come there and said, "Fred, you don't want to talk to no newspaper men." I said, "No, sir." He let me out the back way. The way I went out is the way they transported prisoners in and out of the courtroom. And I went out that way. Daddy signed the bond for me.

Then from April to October I worked with a contractor. Out here on I-65 from Atmore, he was working twenty-five miles of interstate roads. I started off as a laborer and worked them six months and when I quit they tried to hire me for a superintendent. I worked as a laborer and they found out I could operate equipment and I operated equipment for them, and then about the time the trial come up they had about finished the job and all they was doing was a lot of handwork. And the last two months, I guess, I was acting as a foreman for them. I worked a crew of men, a big crew of men for them. I was using my own pickup for their transportation and such as that. Which they furnished my gas, naturally. We worked long hours; I was working sixteen hours a day. Jennie Lee, I'd just come home and I'd just hold my arms up and she'd undress me and I'd just fall right back over in bed. She'd wake me up in six hours and I'd go back up there. After nine years of doing nothing, they like to kill me!

The first day I worked, bear in mind now I hadn't worked any hard, hadn't been out in the sun because, during the time before this happened I worked inside all the time. Went off up there without a hat and had no idea of what I was going to do—but anyway the first job they give me to do was cleaning off a bridge that had twelve inches of clay on it and they had been traveling across it and had also been watering the road on each side of it and naturally they didn't cut the watering truck off and it was like concrete. My hands—didn't have no gloves neither—and that shovel and that sun just eat me up. And I got through with it something like way over in the evening, when dinner time come I didn't do a darn thing but lay down under the bridge, and told this boy that I did know, that lived out here pretty close to here, to wake me up whenever work time come. He said, "Fred you just only get off just long enough to eat." I said, "Well when you get through eating, you wake me up," which was like ten minutes.

I was about dead and about three o'clock the superintendent come up there and got me and told me he wanted me to set some stakes for a motor grader, and what he was doing was clipping shoulders, and that motor grader would run about thirty miles an hour, the stakes was down in a ditch, which the cut was about ten-foot deep, loose dirt, and I was toting a ax and a ten-foot stick in one hand, and I'd have to go down in the ditch and get the stake and bring it up there and lay the ten-foot stick against the pavement was there and drive in a stake at the end of it, and him back there blowing his horn on that patrol telling me to hurry up. And that went on for about seven miles down the road and, so help me goodness, when we got to the end of it he turned that damn patrol around and hauled ass back up the other way and left me standing there, and I had to walk that damn seven miles back down to the other end!

Now, Jennie Lee helped me out of bed the next morning. Shoot, that like to kill me. It took me about two weeks to learn what they done every evening after they knocked off, and what to say and what not to say and in two weeks I made it all right. I worked Wednesday, Thursday, Friday, and Saturday, and then by Monday they had done limbered up a little bit to me.

The crew of men I was working in, they started helping me a little bit there. If they hadn't, shoot, I wouldn't have made it; I would had to quit. Jennie Lee will tell you that.

They knew all about the trouble and everything. And see, the state had inspectors out there, and the Highway Department had inspectors that inspected what they did, and they didn't like them 'cause the workmen would get out there and work like hell for half a day and the inspectors would come in in one of them damned red and black trucks and taking the ground just a little bit, light a fire under a butane burner and heat the dirt a little bit, and then come back and tell him it wasn't wet enough, it was too damn dry, that they'd have to do it all over again. And they didn't like nobody who worked with the Highway Department. Naturally, I found that out quick and I cussed every damn one of them engineers for all kinds of son of bitches in front of them!*

They'd always have a truckload of stuff to go to Columbus, Georgia, that's where their headquarters was, and on Sunday they'd pay me double-time to drive a truckload of stuff up there and unload it; it would take me eighteen hours to make that trip, so you can imagine. Which I would make out there, in one week I'd make might near as much as I made with the state in a month. Awhile ago when I said they tried to hire me, they had a job in California, up in the north part of California, to build a dam which they said would take seven years to build, and this super-intendent that I was under, his name was Wilson, he was going to be the equipment superintendent during the daytime, and they tried to get me to go with him and take care of the equipment at night. Which the pay was something way up yonder, it was fantastic how much money it was. Out there we would have been under the union scale; that's the way the contractor worked. Wherever he worked, he paid according to the union scale, and all my job would have done, all I had a done was like your turn-pulls, your doors, your controls, and all your trucks and every-thing, I would had to see that they greased them and checked and changed the oil in the filters after a certain length of time. Well, I worked with that contractor until the trial.

---

*Jennie: "It didn't help any. Fred still had to walk seven miles!"

At that particular time the civil-rights business was strong; it was hot and heavy. Even one of the jurors wanted to make an example out of us because of it. They said, "Let's send them to the penitentiary to make an example of them, and then no one else will do it." The public opinion was hard against the darn thing. I talked to the prosecutor on the case for the federal government several times after it happened, after it was over with, and he told me that I was lucky. He said, "You don't know how close you came to going to the penitentiary."

I think a lot of it was curiosity to see how we were going to come out of it, too. 'Cause we were the first to be tried. That's why so many people came. Also, most of them was from Clark County from where it happened at. I would say two-thirds of them was people that lived in Grove Hill that knew us personally. Grove Hill was a small town and everybody knew everybody. Then I would say the other third of the people there was people that worked with the Highway Department, that worked with us.

The attorney, or the prosecuting attorney, he started with my daddy. He said, "This is your son, you got a big boy, and from what I can understand by him following in your footsteps.* And Daddy said, "Damn right." Just like that. It passed his tongue before he even thought of what he said. He put Daddy in a kind of bind and hit him with a question, see, and before Daddy could think about it Daddy said he would lie on the stand for me, is what Daddy really said. When he hit him with that and Daddy said "Damn right" I was just brought up in that seat. I said, "Oh, oh!" But what he was on the stand testifying to the fact was—I think I mentioned it, well, I might not have told all of it—but anyway, the confession, remember telling about the confession that the nigger wrote to Daddy? All right, and they had Daddy on the stand, our lawyer did, to testify that this convict did make that statement. Well, they objected to that and the lawyer said he didn't have no more questions for him, and the prosecutor, that's

---

*Jennie: "His purpose was to say, 'This boy's so much like you that you have a special attachment to him and you would get on the stand and say anything to help him, is that not right, Mr. Dees?' "

when he was trying to tear Daddy down—his statement down. That was what he was attempting to do.

Then when Hucklebuck got up there in court, he was on the stand, and me and Mr. Gibson's sitting there in front. Before he ever got started he said, "I want to tell you, Captain Dees, is a good fellow, but he's just doing what he was told to do."

The trial lasted four and a half days. It was a all white, male jury. They went out at eleven o'clock and Daddy said, "Son, if they're back before twelve with a decision, they're going to turn you loose!" And it got on around there to twelve o'clock, they come out and wanted to recess for dinner! And Daddy says, "Son, you're in trouble." But, then when they came back in after lunch they stayed in there ten minutes and came back out and found us not guilty.

I think what happened was—Daddy and Martin Coleman, the man that I said was one of the ones they tried to indict, had a confession that this convict had wrote out. But the judge himself wouldn't let them put that in, wouldn't let our lawyer put that confession in for some reason or another; he kept saying that didn't have nothing to do with the case. But right before, I would say twenty minutes to twelve, the jury demanded to let them have that confession. So the judge brought them back out and charged them to the effect that he was going to let them read the confession, but he didn't want it to have no bearing on the case because Hucklebuck confessed to something that really didn't have no bearing on it because that was a confession to something that we was trying to get him to confess to, but they didn't have us charged with nothing like that. They had us charged with whupping, for using force. And that's what the judge was trying to get them to do, is not use that to throw them off.

On a Friday, before this happened on a Sunday, the post office at Grove Hill got a load of United States stamps. At the post office there hadn't been nowhere like it and the Highway Department bought the whole shipment of this particular stamp, and they was in this little filing cabinet. And after Hucklebuck was transferred to Atmore prison, about three days after then, his girl-friend, that was at Grove Hill, went to the post office and tried to mail a package with some of these stamps. Well, the postmaster recognized them, so the sheriff went out there and questioned her and she said, "Yes sir, Hucklebuck sent me a picture of him and told me in a letter to look in the back of it." And he had mailed her four sheets of them, big sheets of them folded in behind that picture. That was proof right there that he did it. And then several months—two or three months after then—from the time it happened, the river at Jackson, which is twenty miles from Grove Hill, was high, out of the banks. When the river went down, the filing cabinet showed up down there on the banks of the river. He missed the river with it.

I heard Hucklebuck thought he got away with it, but it didn't do him no good. When he got out, he got on a bus for Madison County, and when he stepped off the bus in Madison County he was arrested and sent back to the penitentiary for twenty years. And they likely made the mistake of sending him to me one time!

Fact of the matter, I got—the classification board makes out a list—they make out a sheet. You can get a bunch of new convicts, they classify each convict, and they had a sheet on their names, what they did to them, whether they demoted them or sent them to a road camp, or list them to go to a road camp, and I got a sheet on him, Hucklebuck, saying he was coming to Camp Eight Mile. I wouldn't have done nothing to him.

Afterwards, the people of Grove Hill, they took up the money to pay the lawyer to defend us. And Jennie and I found out about it only by happenstance. The people of Grove Hill, well, Clark County, 'cause it was Clark County, well they made up a little over four thousand dollars for me and Mr. Gibson.* That's the truth. I heard there was more, but I can't prove it. That's what they said. They tried us together, so we just needed one lawyer. Which now, the attorney general's office in Montgomery, they furnished us a lawyer, too. They'd furnished us one, well they did, they sent him down there to help Mr. Coley. Mr. Coley was my lawyer's name who defended me, but the other lawyer was there the first day; the second day he wasn't there.

_____

*Jennie: "The reason we ever found out about it was a man came to Fred and wanted to know why Fred had not thanked anyone for raising that money, and Fred told him we didn't know anything about it."

It was the first time in Alabama anybody was ever tried for whupping a convict—and the last time. It changed the penal system in the road camps a lot. Because up until that point if we had a convict that we couldn't control, we would whup him. And we were supposed to make a report on it, and we was very careless; we didn't see too much sense in making out one. It's part of what caused your officials in the last twenty years to be wishy-washy, we'll take it. Talking about punishing convicts is on account of the public.

Like for instance, up to when they tried me, in the road camps we would just punish a convict without making a report and things like that, and then after they tried us they did try to convict—well they did indict another man, but they never did try him; they finally just throwed it out of court. I think that had a lot to do with the change in the guards' attitude in punishing a convict on his own.

It was something like the next year before I got my back-pay money. We filed a claim against the state, then the state's got a board that handles all their claims, but they just got so much money each year to pay the claims with, and they had been out of money, which over two months; they're always out of money. So this senator introduced a bill before the legislature for them to pay us our back pay and that's how we got it.

Lord, I'm glad that's over.

After the trial I had to go back to work up at Russellville because that's where I was suspended from. And I was supposed to go back—well, I could have went back on the first or something like that—anyway I called them and they told me they had to make a place for me, which I knew that. The personnel board required them to put me back where I was at. And then after I went to work—I worked up there I don't know, six, seven days—and I came home and stayed two, three and went back, and the second time I went back is when Jennie Lee had her wreck.

She was in a automobile wreck on October 30th, just outside Atmore, and I never worked no more in that division. During the time that she was getting over having that wreck, I got a transfer to Eight Mile. The only time I went back up there was when she got well enough to ride. I carried her up there and got my clothes. When they called me, they told me that Jennie Lee had been in a wreck, I left everything I had.

I had been relief steward for that division. I was still a steward, I never was superintendent, but I had acted—during the ten months that I worked at Eight Mile before I was transferred up there, I was acting superintendent. In other words, they transferred me down there. I was number three on the list and, by the rules and regulations, whenever they transferred the superintendent I was working under, they could have sent me up, promoted me, supposed to sent me up; but due to the fact that I was involved in that mess at Grove Hill and didn't know what was going to happen, and back then, like, it was the highway director or assistant highway director, whichever one you want to say, wouldn't let them send me up. Would not let them promote me. And then, after I got out of it and got transferred back to Eight Mile, that's when they promoted me to a superintendent.

The reason I had been boarding at Grove Hill and Jennie Lee was at Atmore was her mother had got sick. Had been real sick. Jennie Lee had been real sick, too, I mean sure enough sick, and the doctor said she didn't need to be by herself much; well the doctor told Jennie along about the same thing, so we decided we'd just move there, and then she'd be with her mother.

Now, my intention had been to stay in Russellville. It was still in the same administration, in other words they had elected, what was the governor before Wallace? Let's see, de Graffenried was running. Who beat Patterson? But anyway, they had already elected him. But this same bunch of people was highway directors, assistant highway directors, and my intention was to work in Russellville 'til the administration changed, but Jennie Lee had the wreck, and the doctor told me again that I would have to be close to her then. If I was planning on going back to north Alabama I'd either better carry her with me, or I could forget about it. So then I went right back to the same people that was against me and they transferred me. I got a letter somewhere that came from the assistant highway director, apologizing to me for what happened—that he didn't understand, that he misunderstood, was misrepresented, a lot of things. He didn't know I had the friends I did, and if he had of knew that in the beginning and all that sort. You know how it goes.

But—then—let's see, I didn't get sent up until June the following year, which was '63. In June of 1963 I went back to Eight Mile as a steward, as a bookkeeper, whichever one you want to call it, and I worked under a superintendent that was a diabetic, the same one they put there after they transferred me to Russellville, fella by the name of Rand. He was a steward, but he was in with the administration, something like twenty-eight on the superintendent's list, and I'm number three. But anyway, I worked something like three, four days, and he got real sick and stayed gone until way after Christmas. Came back and worked a little while and he was off again.

Mr. Logan was resident engineer, and I was running—I was doing the book-work and the superintendent's work. And they was fixing to give the examination again, and that meant that I had to take the examination, get reestablished on the list. I was number three and I had done, after what had happened, I'd done got pretty well disgusted, and one morning I called Mr. Logan, told him to come by the office out there, I wanted to talk to him. Mr. Logan was a good friend of mine, not only the boss man, but he was a damn good friend, still is; he still works down there, but he's stepped up higher. And I told him, I said, "Mr. Logan I don't want to grumble, but," I said, "it's not right for me having to do two jobs," and I said when I should have had it in the beginning. And I said, "Now they're fixing to give me another examination and I might come out of it no telling where on the list," and I said, "it's just not right," and I said, "I want to get off tomorrow." He said, "Why?" I said, "Well, I'm going to Grove Hill and try and get transferred back to Grove Hill." I said, "I feel like if I was at Grove Hill that I would be promoted." And he said, "Well, Fred, you go up there tomorrow, but don't you tell them nothing definite 'til you hear from me."

So, I went to Grove Hill the next day and talked to them and they offered me a superintendent's job, and I told them I would let them know—which they had a opening. And when I got back to Eight Mile the next morning, I hadn't been there ten minutes before Mr. Logan called and told me to come to the office whenever it opened up. At that time we went to work at six, the office opened at eight. (We worked twelve hours; they only worked eight.) And when I got down there he told me that they was going to send me up to do construction work in Mobile County. They had a lot to do, which they did. I done it, but then the superintendent that was over the convict camp, it made him mad, really, because they sent me up. They promoted me, that's what it was, and he, well, he showed his ass, really. He called up the division engineer and told him as long as—well, what they did, they told him that I would be working most of the men, which I had to do construction work, that they wanted him to work with me, and they knew that I'd work with him and we, me and him, together could handle the maintenance work and do the construction. They wanted him to understand that I had priority to any equipment, men, over him.

And it made him mad and he showed his ass, so they called me back down there and told me no, we're not going to put you over construction, hell, we're just going to give you all of it. They told him they wasn't going to cut his classification, which was superintendent, but he would be the steward under me—and he quit. That was in May, we'll say, because they sent me up the 1st of June, I went on the payroll as a superintendent the 1st of June, 1963.

All right, then Mr. Logan, like I said, was a good friend of me. During that time they was buying houses, right of ways to put I-65 through the heart of town. Mr. Logan wanted me to move fast, he wanted me down there as quick as I could move. And I told him it would be a little time because I had to buy a house. He said, "Why buy a house, Fred? Hell, we'll just go out there and find us a damned house on the right of way and jack it up and move it up there and you can live in it."

So, that's what we did. We went down there and got a list of them, they number them all, for auction. And we went over there, it took us about a half a day to find one that I thought I could move. It had to be up off the ground, I figured, and it had to be a solid-built house underneath. And so we found this one, and I never jacked a house up before in my life, didn't even know how. He said, "When you get ready for the truck to haul it, call me." I said, "Well damn, Mr. Logan, I ain't got no jack." He said, "That's right. Wait a minute." He went and called Loxley and called a bridge crew and had them to deliver the jacks over there, to jack bridges up with. I told him I didn't know how to do all that, so he got the bridge crew over here, some of the men to help me, and we jacked it up and moved it. I moved that house up there in about the latter part of October, and then it took me the rest, up until we moved the 1st of January of '64, that's when we moved—it took me that long to get it sat down and all, pour slabs for the porches, build the foundation, septic tanks, painted. I repainted it all.

What happened was, I had it jacked up and I had to go to court for an escape charge the morning that we were going to move it, and I told them, I said, "If we hadn't got it high enough to put that truck under it." I said, "Don't jack it up, it's to get them convicts up under there and dig a row under it." We had it pretty high. A "low boy" is what they haul equipment with; it sets up pretty high and that's what we hauled it on—that's all we had to haul it on, so it lacked something like two inches or three inches. And I got out of court, and I was just all the way out of town, over there at Chickasaw—that's where I got it—I said they ought to be half way up there with it by the time I get over there. I turned down that doggone street and I could see the house and the roof had a big bow in it. They jacked it up on one side and it slid off of the blocks and we had to get up under there and jack it up again! We busted the sheet rock out of it, and it was the next day before we moved it. Took it all day to get it back up.

I stayed there at Eight Mile until they closed the camp. Stayed there for, let's see, closed it in '73, is that the year I said? Up until '75, well, I stayed there two years after they closed the camp.

Yes, I was asked to join the Ku Klux Klan. I have worked with people that I knew was a member, which they said they were, but that's in—you've done got up in the '60s now. R. B. Bryant, I know he was of the what do you call the, well he wasn't the Grand Wizard, but the—you got a Grand Wizard that's over a big section, a big territory; then it's split off into small groups, what they call it? Grand something—he was one of them. He approached me to join, but I couldn't see no reason to. I didn't have no reason to.

At that time, that was in the early '60s maybe, no, that was before the trial. Maybe it was in the '50s, I don't know. It was during the time that the racial problem was coming, was starting, and the Klan tried to use it to get new members and all that in it; if you didn't belong to the Klan and stop the niggers they was going to take over everything, which that's going to happen anyway. Before I die, I'm going to have a nigger boss man, that's just a fact, which don't bother me; I don't give a damn. But that's how fast it's going to change. It's got where now that they can hire one—well, like the Highway Patrol here in Alabama, they have to hire five blacks to every white. If they don't do that the federal government steps in and telling them they're doing it wrong.* No, there wasn't no pressure to join the Klan.

Let's get it down a little bit simpler. Do you know that the average person nowadays that belongs to the Klan, he's nothing in the community, nothing. That's my opinion. Just like R. B. Bryant, he wasn't nothing but a drunkard and about the lowest thing there ever was in Grove Hill. Nowadays, even in the '40s and '50s and '60s I'd say, none of your leaders in the community was a member of the Klan. If they did, if they were, they did it for political reasons, and probably the only ones that knew they was members was the members themselves. It's just the—well, you don't judge a man—probably whenever it was organized, specially in the South, you was, if you wasn't a member they probably looked down on you. But it's turned so much around, if you are a member now they look down on you. It's just in reverse. Shoot, I'd be willing to say in Escambia County—I got no idea how many people live in Escambia County—but if you brought all the Klan members that's in Escambia County you could might near put them in half of this house. It's just not there no more, it's just no reason for it.

The Ku Klux Klan is a bad organization. They had a parade near Mobile here not too long ago, and if it hadn't been for the wives in it they wouldn't have had one. There was so few in it. That's right. I think they just used the wives so they'd have enough

---

*Alabama is under a federal court injunction requiring the hiring of blacks and whites on a one-for-one basis until the percentage of blacks on the state police force reaches twenty-five percent, or the percentage of blacks in Alabama.

for a parade. Robes? Yeah, they just don't cover their face no more, you know it's against the law to cover their face. That's true.

In Alabama, it's dead. They had that rally down at Theodore and it was ridiculous. At Theodore, just on the other side of Mobile. They had a big area of private land that they had designated for it. Had the shotguns and they made speeches about killing niggers and all that; it was something else. I think our area is sick and tired of that kind of—I don't even know the term for it. It's just a thing of the past. What it was all about was; now it's obsolete. Who in hell is going to go out there and pull a nigger out of his house and beat hell out of him, or pull a white man out. Hell, the son of a bitch is liable to kill you now! A guy out there in a white robe. How's he going to get out of the way! And he's burning a cross in front of him! I know damn well I ain't going up to nobody's house in a white robe! Shoot. But now, at the time it was organized, I would say the purpose it was organized for, I would say it served its purpose. But law and order has now taken the place the Klan did.

Same as the NAACP, where your blacks, far as I can see at the time it was organized, for the purpose it was organized, it was good. It was for to get, well let me phrase it like the nigger says, get his freedom. But now, the nigger can't tell you what that means, but what it is, is to quit the segregation. It was to fight it. But now, a nigger or black, whatever you want to say, he's got the same rights that you and I got. It don't make a damn where you sit. But at the time that the NAACP was organized in the South they had four sets of bathrooms, everywhere. The black rode in the back of the bus. Which created attention on that situation, which has now been corrected. And just like your schools, they've put them together. That's what I believe it was all about, which that's what it did, it helped bring that about.

From what I can understand the Klan was organized back yonder after the Civil War when you had what they called carpetbaggers—when they come in here and took the advantage of everybody, and the Klan took the law in their own hands. There was no law, really. There was no way for the law to reach all the people. Except for the few. And it was organized for that purpose, is to, I guess to protect themselves in one sense of the word, which now they got the reputation of hanging niggers, beating hell out of niggers, and even hanging white folks. Maybe they did need hanging, I don't know, but that's the reputation that the Klan's got. And over the years, to get people to join it every time it's any—well, the reason that they chose Theodore to have this rally was because they was having a lot of racial trouble down there at the school, and they figured it would draw a lot of attention and get a lot of new members in it; but it didn't do that. I think it flopped when it come to that. They was trying to raise money, is what they was trying to do.

Another thing that you have to look at about the Klan, when it was organized it—you have to think back in the time element, take like here say, you live here and then maybe, well take this community—well at that time back then you had a sheriff and he was in Brewton. You had one law enforcement, or maybe a marshal over five or six counties. When the Klan was organized. And if something happened in your community it took several days even to get word to the sheriff for him to ever come look at it.

It was secret. It was strictly a secret organization whenever it was organized. You didn't tell nobody that you was a member. From what I can understand, they did a lot of things that was strictly against the law. In fact, they took the law into their own hands, which that's against the law. And for them to protect one another it was, it was just strictly—nobody knew who they were. And they did cover their faces up to where they would not be recognized. And they did that for a purpose, not to be recognized, because they knew they was breaking the law or they wouldn't have covered their face up. And they, I know I've read and I've heard tales all my life about the Klan—ol' nigger over yonder, if he don't straighten up, the Klan's going to come and get him—I ain't never heard of no such thing, I never heard it to be a fact where they did anything.

Today we live in such a faster world that the Klan has got no place in today's time. It's obsolete. It's gone, it's over with. They don't do anything. All they do is march down the street, have a rally, and preach hate—they just preach hate, is all they do. Who listens to it? Usually the man that's talking don't even believe in what he says. He's liable to come off the stand and go into a cheap joint where a bunch of niggers is and have a good time with them. It's just a show, it's just like these wild-west shows that they got aside of the road now to show you what times used to be like, and that's what they do.

What kind of person would belong to the Klan today? He'd be real low. Low on intelligence, he'd be below your average citizen. He would be the type that had been right on the verge of being in the penitentiary. That's strictly my opinion. Now, I could be wrong, but all the members that I know are nothing, really. I don't know if he could be an ex-convict, 'cause I don't know any ex-convicts that's ever been in the Klan. But I'll tell you an organization that's similar to the Klan; it's a new organization. The only difference is, the Klan preaches hate against the blacks, and the Muslims that's coming along here, black power; that's all they teach, is hate against the whites. Same difference, same difference. They're real active. And they're strong, real strong.

The prisons are as integrated today—as much as they can be, let me put it that way. As much as they can be. If the face was red and blue, as long as you got two different type people in any situation they're going to disagree sooner or later. And all the red ones are going to be with the red ones and all the blue ones are going to be with the blue ones. That's strictly my opinion, you're going to always have differences of opinion. Well, it's just like this: say, if you had five brothers out there and I had five brothers out there and me and you got in an argument. Well my brothers going to stand behind me and your brothers are going to stand behind you—that's how simple it is. That's how simple it is.

Another thing now, your penitentiaries are so messed up with your killings which goes on that—I have a man that's on parole now—he's already built two sentences, been in the penitentiary twice—and he says now that he would do anything to keep from going back because of the fear of his life. Another one, Charles Nelson for instance, he says he stayed awake for a month, never shut his eyes, which that—what I'm getting around to saying— that would keep a lot of them from going back. It's just a fear of other prisoners now. They don't have much respect for the guards because they say the guards look to other prisoners to do what they want done. They let the convicts do it for fear of their lives. It was even unheard of even, I never had heard of a convict striking a guard until here recently, much less killing one. Even if a convict cursed the guard back during the time that I was in road camps—that was taboo. That convict would get half killed and quick.

Even a convict, well, I know of one instance where a convict got mad with a guard and he threatened to kill him to another convict and the convict killed him. The convict! The convict killed him 'cause he said if you kill that guard you'll be hard timing us, we'll have to take the punishment of the whole for it; and he killed him, knocked him in the head with a pick. Also now, they've killed several guards up here now in the last year. They work just like the Mafia does that you read about. They pick out the guard they want to kill and then they'll pick a man to kill him, and it's his job to kill him. Usually, *he* winds up dead, too.

The prisoners, they got a certain sense, some of them. They got no hopes of getting out anyway, so he'll take any opportunity; he has to get out. And that's where the people today who're trying to run the convicts, rehabilitate them, now they're spending their time, in my opinion, with the wrong group. The people that can't do nothing, there's no hope for them. They ought to just forget about them and try to help the one that there's hope for. Oh, there's about 20 percent that there's no hope for; that's the one that can put the hat on. They're the ones that's running the penitentiary.

There's another thing, my daddy, he believes in hard work. He said set them out at daylight, back in at dark, and they was tired and they'd go to bed. Well your rehabilitation is more than that; he's got no room for that in his penitentiary. He thinks that Draper is for your first offenders and your younger men; he thinks that's the place that they should do the rehabilitation. The people he had dealt with were hardened criminals, people that had been in two or three times or committed violent crimes, because all the men that was—the majority of them—grand larceny, whiskey charges, such as that, was sent to the road camps, and it didn't leave [him] nothing but the hard men nobody could control, that you couldn't trust him out here at a road camp; and it took, well, you *had* to deal with him with force, really, to get what you wanted out of him. And then they started a rehabilitation in that area, preference to your road camps. I think they would have done, and he does too, done more good if they would have took the men they had out in the fields, you might say, and worked with them, in preference to the ones that was behind the walls. They had been in, say, three or four times, and they had "turned." Well, I could, I could see Daddy's point because I used to, well, I was raised in it. I seen what he had to deal with. And it worked. It worked for him.

The same thing for parole. That's the problem, the parole board never knows as much. You live with a man day in and day out, you become to know him pretty good; but the people that's going to decide if he's going to get out or not are not going to look at your recommendation very much. I know that's just one part of it, but if a man's going to change, if he should change, he should change in ten years. By the same token, a man'll make a good prisoner and he might not make it outside.

The best convict I ever seen was an SB in the streets. I really felt sorry for him, but now he didn't do what I told him to begin with. I paroled convicts, four convicts, at the same time. This particular one, home's in Birmingham, he had to go to Birmingham, and I told him in front of the other three—the other three was local men—I told him, I forget his name, I'll think of it in a minute, "Lookie here, don't you go off there yonder on Davis Avenue and mess around. You go on straight to the bus station and catch you a bus and go home." But, no, he killed time, and then when he got to the bus station it done got dark and way up into the night, and he got the impression that everyone down there was against him. And he called me and wanted me to come get him and put him back in the penitentiary 'til the next morning to where he wouldn't get in no trouble. I talked to him, guess I talked to him for an hour. He was really frightened. I told him to go into the café part of it, sit down and get him a cup of coffee, and just sit there, not to wander outside, and when the bus pulled in, whenever they started loading, for him to go directly and get on the bus. He was scared to death; he thought he was going to get in trouble that night. He apologized for not doing what I told him to do. Not only that, but he was a mess.

Now, today I work strictly with the Highway Department and we don't have any convicts, but I have hired ex-convicts. They was taught road work in prison. Well, actually, another convict taught them usually. These convicts have been in and out and over a period of time they learn how to do all this different type work that we do. Beyond a doubt they work better. The only thing about them, they don't stay very long. Him working right here, doing the same type work he done when he was in the penitentiary, if he can find another job he'll quit it 'cause it's still part of that penitentiary life. He wants to get away from it as quick as he can. And another thing, most of the people that work them now, worked them when they was in the penitentiary. I guess he's got a little chip on his shoulder, 'specially towards some of the foremans that worked him. In some respects there wouldn't be a whole lot of change. They get to go home at night, that's the difference in it, they go home at night. In the crew at Mobile four were at Eight Mile camp when I was superintendent.

Let's see. Harvey White, when he came up for parole, I gave him a job. And then Henry Steppes, now when he got out he's not on parole, he just went free; well eventually, I guess, he couldn't find nothing to do, so he called me and I gave him a job. And then Stanley Benjamin, I gave him a job to get out of the penitentiary to go along with his parole. And then Steve Railton. I gave three of them jobs to make their parole requirements. They wrote me a letter. All of them wrote me a letter, ask me would I hire them when they went up for parole. And I wrote them back and told them I would do it. Three of them colored, one of them's a white boy. Steve Railton is a white boy. Stanley Benjamin has been working the longest, he's been working couple years. White has been working about a year, and Steve's been working about eight months, and Henry Steppes's been working a couple of months.

They can change jobs but they have to ask their parole supervisor can they change, which any time one gets a job better than he's already got—when you say better I'm referring strictly to money, make more money, they'll let him change. He asks his parole officer can he change, and they'll come back and tell you they want to work out a notice.

All three, all four of these worked at Eight Mile. Henry Steppes, he escaped when he was a convict; he stole a truck one night. He was the night cook and he walked out of the kitchen and got him a truck and went riding in it. Other than that, that's the only thing that any of the four ever did.

It's very easy for them to get a promotion, if they would stay, if they would keep working. 'Cause of their knowledge of the road work, they would eventually become a foreman, or a group leader, we call them now. He'd be responsible for a group of men to work. One of them, if I could get an above man to go along with it, I'd make him a group leader now, and that's Harvey White. He's been there next to longest. But I worked him longer in the penitentiary; I worked White straight about five years. White worked with a contractor in the streets, building roads, culverts, concrete work, and that's what I need. I haven't got a concrete man and I'd make him a concrete man if the above man will eventually let me do it. I usually get to do what I want to, change my men around. And he's bright.* He would have that much experience, the experience he had in the penitentiary would count. Same as doing it as a free man.

It was June of '73 was when they closed Eight Mile.

They set a date.

At first when they came, they said they was going to close it, everybody said they was just talking and all that stuff. Let me back up a little bit. Eight Mile is the first camp they ever closed

---

*Fred, Sr.: "He quit before we promoted him. We was planning to promote him, but he quit and took a job that paid more than this one. It was right after Christmas; him and his wife separated, too. Anyway him and his wife separated and him and his daughter got into an argument and she shot him. He was walking away from her and she shot him twice in the head. He died about two weeks after that. He was the most promising. Best worker and all."

Harvey White's daughter was given a five-year suspended sentence on September 27, 1976.

that I know of, and I guess the only one that everybody knew it ahead. Usually when they close one—nobody knew it 'til the morning that they rode up there with the dogwagon to get the convicts. The superintendent, he always knew it, but it was kept quiet to keep down escapes. Which you can understand. A man been in the road camp five, six years, and all of a sudden they going to close it, and maybe he's in a road camp ten, five miles from his home, and he's been there, you know, and got used to it, but it would upset him, just like if you lived in a house a long time and somebody come along and force you to move; well, they've got feelings that way too.

They told everybody, which I lost a lot of convicts right there at the last on account of it. They did escape. Shoot, I had more escapes from the time that they found out that they were going to close that thing, had more escapes in something like three months than I had in four, five years, or longer.

Fact of the matter, I just now, two weeks ago, went on the last escape charge. What happened was he escaped and he had just a little time and he wasn't tried in that length of time and when he built his time out they picked him up and brought him back to Mobile and he made bond on the escape charge. It was a new offense, so they let him make bond, and then he jumped bond and he stayed gone all this time up until here recently, and they caught him and then they had to try him again, and that's the reason they called me down there as a witness against him. The man that he escaped from, he done died. I was the only witness. The guard that he was with, checked out to, was working him, he had died. But they not only had him on a escaped charge; him and another one stole a truck, then went and robbed this filling station with a Coca Cola bottle—they had him on that, too. Robbery. What they did, they really passed over the escape and the grand theft and tried him on the robbery charge. The boy that he robbed was there as a witness. He got ten years is what he got.

They gave something like three months notice, is the best I can remember; they knew it three months before it closed. They all went to another road camp except three. It was forty-two men left there, it was forty-two men there the day they came after them, and they had papers to transfer all forty-two of them to other road camps. The way they did it, they went right down the line, alphabetical order, and transferred the first ten to this road camp, the next ten to that, and the five, three, and so on. Except three of them now. Mr. French, which he had the authority to do it, I told them if those three—I picked them out and give him their records—if you want to save somebody a lot of headaches, you ought to send these three to Atmore. I said if you send these three to another road camp, I said all you're doing is just sending headaches there. And he took me as my word and transferred them three to Atmore. I had forty-two and we transferred thirty-nine to other road camps. I don't remember how many escapes were still out, it wasn't no great amount, it must have been like maybe two, maybe three. But now, they have been caught since then.

I went there one time, during the time I was running it, the best I remember, something like eighteen months in between escapes. That was when I first started running it. And then your penitentiary, your convicts started changing, your attitudes and all that, and your new ones started changing. I had maybe two, three in some years, and maybe I had four, but I don't believe I ever had more than seven in a twelve-month period until the last year. The best I remember there was nineteen left there—no, that's too high, there wasn't that many. The last year, which in three months that they knew they was going to close it, I think the best I remember, eight run in them three months, and I lost eight convicts after they told them they was going to close.

Not only did I lose eight convicts, but I had to transfer ten or twelve back that just went crazy—well not crazy, but they just went wild. They had been good convicts up until they said, "Well, I ain't got but three more months here, so I'll do like I want to"— you know how that is. Just like you was finishing high school or something. Those went back to Atmore. I had that escape report in my hand the other day. I had it in the truck because nobody else had any use for it but me, and the reason I kept up with it is on account of this boy I was telling about. I knew sooner or later I had to go to his trial, and you get down there and you can't remember all the details, what time he left and all of that, who he was with and exactly the details of it; and I kept it for that pur-

pose, where I could refer back to it if I got a subpoena. And the
other evening when I left, I got it out of the pocket of the truck
and I put in my personal truck. I laid it on the seat of the truck.
I said, "Hell, I believe I'll carry that home with me because nobody else has no use for it. Just really a dead record now." And
I said, "No, something might come up," and I carried it back in
the office and give it back to them and told them to put it where
they could put their hands on it if I ever needed it. If I had it, I
could tell just like that how many. So there's three years' escape
reports in it.

Which, they going to close them all. That's something that
happened recently, they got orders to shut every one of them
down. By the first of January, 1976.*

Now, the camp at Grove Hill is a new one, it's a gun camp. Now
they're going to let the Board of Corrections have it, that's one
that the Highway Department is going to—what they're going
to do with the convicts, I don't know 'cause I don't think the Highway Department is going to work them. But the Board of Corrections is going to have to take the building over and probably
operate it as a work-release camp. Is the new system.

The Board of Corrections, the new people which has come in,
say the road camp has no rehabilitation towards the inmates, it
doesn't help them any. They don't rehabilitate them anyway,
so they say it's best for them not to be in a road camp. Actually,
the road camp kept them more up-to-date on what was going on
in the streets 'cause they was in the streets with the people. They
knew how to deal with the people, the public, 'cause that's the
kind of work they did. And they would learn, as time changed in
the street, they would learn the changes that was made. Now,
when they pulled him back and put him in the penitentiary, he
doesn't know nothing about what's going on outside the penitentiary.

If there was violence in the road camps, you don't never read
about it. And if it was, you would read about it. Well now, let's

---

*At this writing (January, 1977), there have been proposals to convert
some of the road camps into work- or early-release centers, but no
definitive policy for their use has as yet been set.

just back up a little bit. That's one of the reasons they started closing the camps, because they had two instances of violence. And they used that to close two of them. The closest one here is Grove Hill, and even escapes, we hear that on the two-way radio when they have one, and it's very seldom that I hear them talking about an escaped convict.

Reopening the road camps would eliminate it all. The overcrowding. Not only would it eliminate, but instead of them begging for the legislature—which has just appropriated them more money than they ever had—putting them back in the road camps would give them a income way up in the millions of dollars, plus would help the Highway Department, in my opinion.

In the Highway Department they done got now where we're working under a strict budget and they ain't got no money. The personnel is cut way low, and I still say, and will always say, that you can run a convict camp, work the highways, have more people working, do a better job cheaper than you can hire free people to do it. By opening the road camps you would serve two purposes. It would help the Highway Department 'cause it would give them more people to work on less money, and help the overcrowding problem.

More convicts are being held in county jails. Inside, no exercise; it's locked up. They're having pure hell in Mobile. They're just having riots one right after the other on account they're overpopulated, they're overcrowded. I've read several articles here lately in the Mobile paper where the sheriff, he just don't know what the heck he's going to do with them. Then you got Fall Court coming up. These small towns like Brewton, county seats, they don't have court but twice a year, Spring Court and Fall Court. In Mobile they have it all the year, but these small counties, their log of cases builds up, and then all over the state—if you get five from each county, times the counties—which is sixty-seven or seventy, or whatever it is, sixty-nine, I believe, say seventy—if you get five from each county that's three-hundred and fifty. That's a lot of convicts when you put them together.

Instead, they're closing the road camps at a time when they could take the overflow of prisoners. But, the thing is, the build-

ings that they are in are owned by the Highway Department, and
each road camp is a district headquarters, which most of them
cover a whole county; some cover two counties. The Highway
Department needs that space to carry on their operations, specially the office and such as that. That's in front of a road camp,
that part of it. Once you move the convicts, that part of it don't
quit; they still have to have a office space and a warehouse and a
place for the men to meet in the morning to work. When they
close a camp that means they have to hire people to report in the
same place that the convicts worked out of, for them to do the
work that the convicts was doing. The buildings that they are, if
they gave them to the Board of Corrections the Highway Department would have to build new buildings to handle their business.
Their operations, whichever one you want to call it.

It's hard, it would be hard if I was governor to say to the Highway Department, "Give all your property to the Board of Corrections to handle convicts with." If you did that, well, all the
convict camps, it's just like that one down yonder at Eight Mile,
all the material that we use is stacked around it, you'd have to
move all that out of the way to another location. Really and truly,
the buildings itself would be a fine place for even to take care of
say a hundred, and there's ten of them, so that'd take care of a
thousand convicts. You could put them in there, well actually you
could hold them there just as good as you could in a county jail—
more so, because a convict camp is equipped more to take care of
them, if they would screen them. They'd have to be screened
because some of them you couldn't hold in a convict camp; they'd
tear out of the damned thing. You'd have to do a little adjusting.
You'd have to get some out of the penitentiary that would stay in
a place like that, say minimum security; you could class them like
that. You got that many in that you could put in a place like that.

To boil it down plain and simple, the penal system in Alabama
is in a heck of a mess. Just like I said a while ago, the legislature
has appropriated, I don't know, a million dollars, that they have
given them extra this year, and some of it is to build new buildings, but you don't stick a building up over there overnight. It
takes a while to build a penitentiary. A penitentiary you can figure
three or four years to build it. They're caught right in between,

and you take—the legislature met in January, 1975, I guess is when they started—and they didn't pass no money until the last night they was up there for either the Highway Department— didn't even pass none for the Education Department, for the school board.

George Wallace had to use his authority to operate on last year's budget for them; they didn't even appropriate any money for the Board of Education. They gave the prison system a lot of money. For one thing, they give them all the money that the license plates take in, which amounts, I think, to two million dollars extra from what the budget was. Their budget comes out of the general fund and they did give a budget on it, but they cut them fifteen million dollars short from what they asked. They asked for fifteen million more than they got, just to operate on, and they cut them fifteen.

So you see they wanted a lot of money to match some federal funds to finish the Interstate like 65 across the river over here, and they said they'd give them enough money to operate and they already laid off some people, and I heard again they're going to lay off some more because they haven't got enough money to operate on from this budget they're getting.

I don't know what's going to happen. I really don't know. I worked with them all these years and I've never seen—Daddy will tell you the same thing, all the years he worked, he never seen anything like this.

Can't get nobody to work.

The federal government issued a whatever* they do and told them if they didn't straighten the penal system up by a certain length of time that they would be forced to take it over, and I guess that would be the next step, for them to take it over. They give them so many days to correct the overcrowding and such as

---

*On August 29, 1975 U.S. District Judges Frank M. Johnson, Jr., of Montgomery and William Brevard Hand of Mobile ordered Alabama to stop accepting any new inmates at four state prisons until the populations dropped to the levels for which the prisons were built. The judges ruled on a suit filed on behalf of inmates of the state prison system.

that. I don't know the length of time they gave them. They've had two or three cases where the convicts themselves, due to overcrowding, they would sue them, or file a what's it called? I don't know whether it was in the paper or not, but they had a big one at Mt. Miegs, the receiving center. They had to call in the highway patrol and all to separate the colors, the blacks from the whites, and kept them that way for awhile, and the federal government gave them so many days to put them back together and they put them back together and they had another one. Riot—blacks and the whites fighting against one another. And they said that was due to overcrowding.

Daddy's idea of a penal system that would work was one that would be self-supported. My idea of a penal system that would be successful would be to let each county handle their own penal systems. Not have them go to the Board of Corrections. Instead of the state having a Board of Corrections, the revenue that the Board of Corrections gets, split it up amongst the counties, according to size, and let each county operate their own penal system. Let each county be responsible for their own penal system. Let them have their own farm, let them worry about their own welfare of the convicts.

The only drawback to it would be politics. They would have them some system or another to always have qualified personnel, to not let county politics enter into the penal system. They got county convicts, but they keep them in the county jails. But that's my idea of the best penal system. Mobile County, for example, the sheriff department there is so large that they got their own penal system. I would imagine Birmingham is the same way.

But, now, you take Baldwin County here, the sheriff's race is on now. If the sheriff goes out, gets beat, a new sheriff comes in, he would change the whole law-enforcement personnel. He wouldn't keep any of them. He would put his own people in. That's the way the sheriff gets to pay back political debts. What I am saying now is if they would let each county handle their own convicts, have their own system according to the size of the county, and take them in, part of them, and raise their own food, and take it and put each one of them under the same merit system, that would take it out from under the sheriff or the probate judge, or who it might be, and put it under a system. If you was a warden and a sheriff changed in a county you would have a guarantee of a job, and you could get personnel.

The reputation of the Alabama prison system? The public thinks that the system is bad. They say sing to the mighty convict and look down on a guard. A convict gets killed, the papers play it big. A guard gets killed, you have to look hard in the newspaper to find it. For instance, the first one that got killed, they printed in the paper a lot about the convict himself, which he was killed too, and very little was said about the guard. That was at Atmore. Looking down on the guard.

I had a judge the last trial I had to go to on an escape, after they closed this camp. It was in Mobile, and the judge turned the convict loose, found him not guilty of escaping—and that's the *easiest* thing to prove, is that he escaped! Anytime that he leaves the sight of the guard he's escaped because that's the rule, that's it. But anyway, they had the trial and questioned the guard and questioned me and the convict and then the judge leaned over to me and told me that he was just going to have to let that convict go on the escape charge—that due to the type personnel I had down there testifying. He said, "My advice to you is to hire you some better personnel." Now, he actually told me that.

There's no fear of cruel punishment, not from the guards' standpoint, but from the convicts in them now more so then— used to be from the guards years past—fear from them. But now it's the fear from the convict himself. Convict control.

Their point about the whole situation is with the public, society; you got an element in there that the public don't know. That's why 10 percent or 20 percent that's in there that there's no control, no hope for him whatsoever. The only chance of him getting out is to escape—because he'll never get out, his record is so bad and he is a violent, violent person.

Well, that's the type people. What they have done, they've kept that man locked up all the time; he's never seen daylight. They kept him away from the other inmates because the people

knew, the guards, or the man's warden, or whoever it was running the prison, knew the situation. The public and organizations
like Link* has caused so much criticism that the penal system
was forced to let that man out. The federal government, too, had
a lot to do with it, pressure on it. And they had to let him back
out amongst the inmates. Well, now that's the element that's got
control over your penal system within the prison, and the guards
know that. The people that's worked and got the experience,
they know what's happening, but nobody will listen to them.
They've sold the public, the guards are the bad guys.

Now, I can't understand them hiring women. They got where
they're hiring—well they got a case now, I heard over the news—
for "security counselors," they call them; they don't call them
guards no more. They got a certain height, weight on the quali-
fications, and two women, according to the news, filed a suit to
get that requirement lowered. And they [the Board of Correc-
tions] went on and said that the reason is that that requirement is
there is for self-protection—that at any time you might have to
protect yourself. Something, like the weight was a hundred and
sixty pounds. Minimum height is five-six, five-eight, something
like that. The bad part about it, the women are making more on
the examination. Scoring higher on the examination than the
men are.**

I'll tell you, your convict guards or counselors, whatever you
want to call them, what they call them now, they done about

---

*Fred, Sr.: "Link means the link between the convict and his family.
The Link Society, in my opinion, was more interested in trying to tell
the Board of Corrections how to run the penitentiary. They got into
this big thing about being conned. Like they got a file over there, it's
nothing but critical letters from convicts about the penitentiary, and
they eat that stuff up. They read them and then they want to go back to
the warden and dig at him about such as that, which they're doing themselves more harm than if they would take the money that's allotted to
them and work between the convict and his family. They would accom-
plish a whole lots more."
**On June 27, 1977, the United States Supreme Court struck down
Alabama regulations imposing height-and-weight standards for prison

played out. A man that's got a little education, he don't want to go up there and risk his life in that thing. Since all this turmoil has come along and your guards has done got killed up there and cut, well you'd think a long time before you'd go to work up there. Even myself, I'd think a long time before I'd go to work up there. Because I know this, it wouldn't be but just a little while, they might hire me as a guard and put me out there on the shack, but it would be just a little while before they'd pull me and put me inside there. In the manner of things, I'd think a long time before I'd run that risk of getting messed up. They're even asking now for extra pay now, like the police force has got, hazardous pay. They got a bill in now that they ought to pay the guards up there, which they're right.

And the guards in the past, they would hire guards just any time that they wanted some. They had a list, get a guard any time. Now they can't hire nobody. But if a guard lost a convict, he lost his job. And that makes a lot of difference. And then back then a guard's job was a good job. The pay scale back then wasn't nothing, but nobody else had anything. Actually he was making pretty good money. He got a house furnished to him, vegetables furnished to him, and milk furnished to him, meals furnished to him, and he could raise all the meat he wanted to. All the feed was free, so what money he made was clear. He had nothing to buy except flour; his eggs was furnished to him, too.

It's a different game being played now, though. What you're doing there, you put a piece of dynamite in your pocket, and that's what you walk around with. Just any time it's liable to go off.

---

guards as violating federal laws that prohibit sex discrimination in hiring. However, the court upheld an Alabama regulation effectively prohibiting women from serving in "contact" jobs at the state's maximum-security prisons.

3 FRED H. DEES, JR.

The "new breed" of probation/parole

officer looks at rehabilitation and life

after prison.

Fred Dees, Jr.

We talked in his office, a

windowless cubicle that lends nothing to the spirit of a man, in a grey building that adds little to its surroundings other than to take up space. That's the nature of courthouses and probation offices—depressing but practical. Mesmerizing, colorless walls and a blank desk fill the gap between probation officer and criminal. It is an effort to speak or listen; the slightest cough is a momentous intrusion and distraction. Fred Dees, Jr., met there one morning to instruct a young man on the rules of probation, and it was in this atmosphere that he first spoke of the Alabama prison system, its strengths and weaknesses, and what he hoped for.

In the course of one conversation, in the midst of an idea, he summed up his philosophy:

"The only thing I feel like I can do is show them the alternatives: if you do this, there's a good chance you'll go to prison; or if you do this, you're going to lose your job. If you do this, eventually it's going to catch up with you and you won't get anywhere. I deal mostly with just alternatives."

At twenty-five, Fred is the third in line of Dees men to be involved in Alabama correctional work. He is the first to graduate from college. To describe him is, in some ways, to describe his father: most valuable lineman for the Vigor High football team in the mid-'60s, soft-spoken, personable, introspective. And, like his father, Fred did not plan to enter his chosen career. But there the similarities end.

When he entered college Fred's principal academic interest was history. Later, he combined a major study in political science with one in criminal justice. Now, he is pursuing a master's degree in corrective counseling, and he has helped establish Mobile's first federally funded halfway house exclusively for probationers and parolees.

Fred deals with the criminal, or ex-convict, from a different perspective than those of his grandfather and his father before him. His is outside the prison and relies on neither fundamental discipline nor pragmatic control; he adds a third dimension.

"I take the nondirective approach . . . more or less just trying to talk with him, lead him, and show him."

Fred H. Dees, Jr.

"Moses Hampton. Go ahead and have a seat right there. Moses, like I told you last week, the reason you're coming down here today is to go over your rules of probation. Now, which should be relatively easy 'cause you already know them, since you're on probation now for a previous offense. Did you understand fully what happened in court? Last week?"

"I know they told me I was on six-months probation."

"Well, you're on two-years probation."

"Two?"

"Yeah, the judge sentenced you to six months in the county jail and he suspended that for two years. Now, you realize yourself why you had such a long probation period, don't you?"

"Ah, why, this time? Yes."

"Well, I've talked to you a lot of times in the last three months about the fact that you're on probation for assault and battery, and you got arrested for a new marijuana offense. Even though your probation was fixing to go off here next month, Judge Holt, who put you on probation to start with, thought maybe it would be best that if he didn't revoke your probation—that you'd at least be continued on probation. Well, the way I understand it, Judge Harrington knew that, too, and that's the reason he placed you on probation for two years. That's the main reason you got such a long sentence. And like I told you last week, before you went to court, Judge Holt still hasn't said anything definite about whether or not he's going to revoke your probation. The main reason is because you still have that other marijuana case pending, and I believe you go to court on it Friday, don't you?"

"Monday."

"Monday? Have you talked to your attorney any more about that?"

"Yeah."

"Okay. I can't tell you anything definite on that until that case is disposed of. It won't affect this probation, but it will affect the one Judge Holt imposed on you. Two years ago. So, mainly I need to go over these rules with you. And I want you to under-

stand fully that you are on probation for two years. Now, I believe
Mr. Lander, the other probation officer, explained all the probation rules to you once before, didn't he?"

"Yeah."

"Okay. And, as far as I'm concerned you complied with them
all except for these new arrests. Now, the first condition here is,
you're to avoid injurious or vicious habits. I'm sure when Mr.
Lander explained to you once before, he told you that means
that any habit or any behavior on your part that is likely to get
you in trouble or to interfere with your job, your home life, or
anything in that respect, such as staying out late at night, drinking
to excess—in other words it covers a lot of ground and it's open
to me to decide if you've violated it. I'm sure you have a pretty
good idea yourself of what it means. It also means, Moses,
that you're to obey the law. Now, I went over and over with you
about the importance of letting me know when you get arrested,
which you didn't on any time, even on that possession of marijuana or that assault and battery. You know that yourself, you
didn't call me and let me know, you didn't get any word to me at
all. Like I told you once before, the reason I want you to let me
know about it, I need to get your side of what happened.

"Just like in this possession of marijuana case, if you'd called
me and let me know what happened, you know, give me the
details right after you got arrested, I would have looked at it in
a little different light. But you didn't call me, and I didn't know
what in the world was going on 'til I saw your name come up on
the court docket over this. Now, you've been given a break, so
far, as far as this rule goes on your probation. Now, I think when
Mr. Lander instructed you, I'm sure he told you that everybody
has to obey the law. I have to obey it, everybody does. The only
difference is, you have to do it a little bit better than everybody
else. You got a little more hanging over you than everybody else.
And a word to the wise, if you do get arrested again, I would say
the chances are real good that you will go to jail; your probation
will be revoked and you'll have to serve that six months in jail.

"The other condition is you're to avoid persons or places of
bad reputation or harmful character. Now again, that's pretty
general, there's no way I can look over your shoulder every day

and tell you no, you're not to associate with him, no you can't be seen with that one, that one's okay. That's something you're going to pretty well have to decide for yourself, you know. You pretty well know who your friends are, which ones been in trouble before, which ones are always talking some crap about breaking the law or using drugs or what not. So, it's going to be up to you.

"This same situation came up when you got arrested for possession of marijuana. You know yourself, even though you didn't have the thing with you, you were with somebody or you got in a situation where you shouldn't have been. So that's something you're going to definitely have to avoid. As far as places, you're to stay away from any place where drugs are being sold or used or you have any idea they're there at all. That means a club, a house, a car, anything. Also, you're to stay away from any clubs where alcohol is sold and that's pretty self-explanatory. It doesn't mean a grocery store or something, but it does mean club.

"You're to report to the probation officer as directed. Now, I'm sure you're pretty familiar with that; I know you know how to fill out a monthly report. You can come in once a month, like you always have, between the first, second, third and fill out a report. Now, if you move or change jobs, you call me and let me know right away. Don't wait around until the first of the month and tell me on the report.

"All right, you're to permit me to visit you at your home or elsewhere. I'm sure you know how that goes, too. And you probably know the reason we come out there. One is to see if you're working like you say you are, and see if you're living where you say you are. And the second is to see how things are going with you—that's the most important one. See if you have any problems with anything. Now, you definitely look for me to come out to your house once a month. You're to work faithfully at suitable employment as far as possible, and that's self-explanatory. Now, you have a pretty good job now, don't you Moses?"

"Yeah."

"What's your boss' name?"

"The foreman?"

'Yeah."

"Reverend Jones."

"Is he a pretty good man to work for?"

"Yeah."

"Is he pretty good or could be better?"

"He's all right."

"Does he treat you pretty good while you work?"

"Yeah."

"What kind of work are you doing?"

"Ah, I'm, ah, working out on the streets, edging."

"Edging curbs?"

"Yeah."

"Pretty good people to work for? I mean the other people on the crew?"

"Ah, yeah."

"Now, Moses, if you ever are out of a job, let me know about it and we'll make arrangements to find you another job. You know yourself you didn't always let us know during the last two years if you weren't working. The only time you'd let us know was when you'd fill out your report. I don't know why you didn't call us— did you think we were going to get on to you?"

"Get on to me?"

"Get on to you or give you a hard time 'cause you weren't working?"

"Well, I like to go find another."

"So, you pretty well like to do things for yourself, as far as finding a job? Do you think you can do it better that way rather than somebody helping you? But, you didn't have luck that way all the time, did you?"

"What, finding a job?"

"Yes."

"Ah, I found a job here every time I looked."

"Well, did you put on some of your reports some months you didn't work that month?"

"Ah, yeah."

"Did you think maybe that if we had been helping you find a little more steady job, maybe like the one you got now, things would have worked out a little better?"

"Yeah."

"But, you never called us. Did Mr. Lander tell you that if you were ever out of a job to call us, get in touch with us?"

"Yeah."

"You just thought we meant pretty well on your own go find a job as long as you had one?"

"That's it."

"Okay. From now on, if you're out of a job or if you think you need something a little better or something that pays a little more, get in touch with me. I'll definitely help you try to find something. I can't, you know, can't promise I will but we'll sure look around and see. The next condition, Moses, is you're to remain in a specified place as directed by me. You understand, you're not to leave the state of Alabama unless you have my permission? As far as leaving Mobile County, if you're leaving Mobile County and going somewhere else in Alabama and you're only going to be gone, let's say one day, you can go ahead and go. If you're going to be gone for more than one day you need to call me and let me know, and if you've got a good reason for going I'll give you permission. All right, you're to support any dependents you have to the best of your ability. Now, Moses, you're not married, are you?"

"No."

"And, you're still living with your mother, aren't you?"

"Yeah."

"Do you help her out with finances some? Are you able to?"

"Yeah."

"About how much do you give her a month? Or does it vary?"

"Ah, thirty-five, fifty."

"That pretty well every month? Well, I know she appreciates that, you being able to help her out a little around the house. The last condition, Moses, is you're to pay court costs by June the 12th of this year. Did you have to pay court costs on that other case?"

"By next month."

"Next month? Well, this is your cost bill. Now, you know you pay your court costs to a certain clerk's office."

"That's downstairs?"

"No, it's on this floor, down the hall. Down by the district attorney's office. Now, they won't take partial payments; you have to pay it all at one time. You got until this date to pay it—that's sixty days. If you haven't got it by that date and you don't let anybody know, well they're going to issue a warrant for you. The best thing to do is try and save up your money or wait until you get paid right before the 12th and come down here and pay it. Now, they won't take a check, you'll have to pay it in cash. If something comes up or you get sick and you're not able to work or something, get in touch with me and I'll try to get you some more time on it. But if you don't let me know, now, and you don't get paid, I'm telling you they're going to issue a warrant, and it'll be out of my hands then. In other words, the judge is the one that issues it.

"Moses, that's the conditions. Now, there shouldn't be any excuses on your part if you come up later and I see that you've violated one, and then you say I didn't know about that one, 'cause this is your second go-around on probation and you oughta pretty well know the ropes now. And the few things I think you don't understand, I'm going to ask you to get in touch with me when you're having problems or something.

"You know yourself, here during the last, well since Christmas time when you got arrested for this, you didn't let me know anything. I had to call you, I had to go get you to find out what happened. And you know yourself if somebody did something wrong and then didn't let you know, the first thing that comes into your mind is that they're trying to hide it. Isn't that right? So let me know about it; if you have any problems, you know, don't be afraid to call me. You may not think that's what they pay me for, is to help you stay out of trouble—help you stay out of prison. So, be sure and let me know about it.

"Now, when you go to court Monday, come back over here and see me. Like I said awhile ago, I don't know what Judge Holt's going to do. I would imagine that he's just going to let your probation run out. But, you'll still have this other two years to do. To be frank with you—and you know yourself—my contact with you, and every time you came into this office, it hasn't been for anything good, has it? About every time you came in I've had to get on to you. I don't enjoy doing that. I know you don't, and I wouldn't either if I came to see you every time and you jumped on me every time I came in. But, this is going to give us another chance to change that.

"You got one more card, you still got it Moses? You going back to work today?"

"Still got it."

"You off the job? For tomorrow? What days you working? Or did you just have to take off today? What time do you usually get off?"

"Three o'clock."

"Okay. I want you to remind me now every time I set an appointment for you to come in, you stop me and tell me you've got to work and you can come in after three o'clock. Okay? 'Cause if you don't tell me I'll forget about it and cause you to miss a day of work. Okay, Moses, I'll see you Monday then. Like I said now, if anything comes up, like it did the last time, call me and let me know about it. Now, I'll see you Monday."

Wish I could have got him to open up. He's just that way. But, like I told him, every time he came in here I got on to him about something, and I guess he's just used to sitting there and taking it. I got him about November, I guess. He had been Lander's, and then Lander transferred and I took over. Well, I had a small case load and I took his over, too. I had about one hundred and fifty, and I took his, too. Moses was one of his.

This is what—this is the probation he's on now—what happened:

Moses William Hampton, black male, twenty-two. On December 18, 1973, Hampton was arrested by Mobile police officers and charged with petty larceny and assaulting a police officer with a deadly weapon. On December 20, 1973, subject appeared in the Mobile Municipal Court and was found guilty of petty larceny. He was observed picking up a man's cap valued at three dollars and ninety-seven cents from a counter and concealing it under his jacket. The police officers followed him out of the store; the subject reached the parking lot of the store and Officer Sanderson apprised Hampton he was a police officer and he was under arrest. Officer Sanderson states the subject pulled a knife and attempted to strike him. As Hampton turned and ran, Officer Sanderson shot subject in his leg. Hampton was then transferred to Mobile General for treatment of gunshot wounds in his right and left legs and a hold was placed against subject, charging him with petty larceny and assaulting a police officer with a deadly weapon.

A search of the area by Mobile police officers failed to disclose the knife. He claimed that he was innocent. Subject said he tried on the cap in the store but did not steal anything. Subject states that the arresting officer approached him in the parking lot and began cursing and accusing him of stealing the cap. Subject stated that the officer dared him to run so he could shoot him. Hampton states he panicked and ran. Hampton denied he struck at officer with a knife or that he even carried a knife.

There was a trial, a hearing. He was ordered to pay a fine of one hundred and twenty dollars, and serve sixteen days in jail. But he appealed at the same time. He later explained to me, at the hearing they reduced to disorderly conduct and a fine of fifty dollars or something.

I've tried to talk to him about it; I didn't have to go into any details. Normally, I would have. Let's see, he's got a new one here; this is the one coming up in court Monday, that's charge two. Here's his presentence, that's the other charge he's got pending. That's the reason, see, I'd recommended when this came up on these charges that the details were a little vague. I honestly believe that I'm sure Officer Sanderson was quite belligerent with him. Knowing Officer Sanderson that fits him to a "T." He is just, I mean, just obnoxious. Moses probably stole the cap, and it's hard to believe he didn't carry a knife.

He was originally arrested in December for allegedly stealing a cap, and then on March 2, 1974, there was a new arrest for possession of marijuana. He was out on trial, made bail. He was on an appeal bond originally, and then he was released before this possession of marijuana on a bond of five hundred dollars. In his case there's very little chance he's going to run off.

March 2, 1974, approximately three-thirty A.M., Mobile police officer C. B. Hendricks stopped a vehicle at Government Boulevard and Washington Avenue for a traffic violation. All occupants of the car, four black males, were ordered out of the car, and after producing identifications were told to leave. At this time the officer observed subject picking up something near the car. After the officer questioned Moses concerning this, he noticed subject put his left hand down near the floorboard of the car and dropped a cigarette, but which appeared and smelled similar to marijuana, and a white capsule.

Hampton was then arrested for possession of marijuana and all evidence was turned over to the state pathologist for examination. Hampton stated to this supervisor that on the night of the offense he was riding with a friend on Davis Avenue. Hampton states that his friend stopped to pick up three other black males, one of whom appeared to be smoking marijuana. Hampton further contends that this unknown male dropped his cigarette butt on the floorboard and got out of the car shortly before the arresting officers arrived.

That's pending, comes up Monday in Municipal Court. On this one, his story doesn't sound too good. First of all, he shouldn't have been on Davis Avenue. Davis Avenue, it's the main drag through the black area in Mobile, and from one end to the other, clubs, and it's where all the heroin traffic is, and among the blacks that's the main place it's going to originate. Has a very bad reputation. He didn't have no business there. Besides, his juvenile record goes back to 1967, disorderly assembly; city vagrancy, 1971; assault and battery, 1971; disorderly conduct, 1971; burglary second degree, 1972.

Now, the assault and battery was dismissed and the others were *nolle prosequi*, they weren't prosecuted. In Moses' case, I went out on a limb for him on this first one, this assault and battery with the police officer, because there were a few things that just didn't fit. There's some question as to whether the officer might have provoked him to start with, and I wouldn't doubt that at all. Well, he might have stole the cap. Anyway, after I did that, it comes out he gets arrested for possession of marijuana. Well, I'd waited too long then, since I'd already recommended to the judge he not do anything, and he comes up on a new case before Judge Holt and he said, "Boy, what do you want me to do?," and I said, "Well, since he's gone this far, if the possession of marijuana case is *nolle prosequi,* I recommend we continue him on probation for a couple of years, and if he gets into anything else, sure—any deviant behavior at all." He said okay, but in between that, what they did, instead of continuing this probation, when he came up on the assault and battery, they just went ahead and put him on probation for that, and probably he goes off on it the tenth of next month; so let it expire and they can put him up on this other one—the marijuana. I doubt seriously they're going to revoke him now. This possession of marijuana was only pending, so you can't revoke him on a pending case. If he's convicted of it—which I'm sure it will be possession of marijuana for personal use, which is a misdemeanor—if he's convicted on it, Judge Holt might revoke probation. But I doubt it, I doubt it seriously.

It worried me when I first started talking to him, because he would never open up, he'd never say anything, so I thought I'm just not reaching him, there's no way I can talk to him. I'm doing something wrong, I need to try something else. So I went to his attorney. He's young, and long hair, and had a good relationship usually with his clients, and he usually handles drug cases. I went and talked to him, and he said he had the same problem with him and he's worried about it, too.

Of course, he's in a little bit of a situation, and he said he's never been able to get him to talk about it. His mother says he talks all the time, so the main thing I believe the problem is because the first few times I had contact with him, had to get on him, you know, every time, and I was seeing him maybe two, three times a week, and he steadily got to the point where he talks less and less. I'm going to have to try and do something, build some kind of relationship with him; which could be simply because I'm white and he's black, I'm going to have a hard time.

A funny thing about that, though, getting off the subject a little bit, we've got a black probation officer now, and he's got a black area, and we all thought he's going to get right in—he'd have a relationship right off. He had as much trouble as we did. But, on Moses, he's straddling the fence now, and he's been given a lot of breaks. Usually they don't get that many chances.

Another thing in his favor is the judge he's got. Judge Holt is the type—he's very funny—if you stand and joke with him, he won't send you to the penitentiary. If you want him sent off, he'll put him back on, he's not consistent with anything. His main problem is he can't remember anything, but he is getting old. Tell him one thing, you work something out with him, then go to court and he does something else. There's no consistency to him. Any other judge would send Moses up the first time, I'm sure of it. So, that's what I've been faced with. Moses might think, well I got off of this and they've let me get by on this one too, so what the hell, I ain't doing anything.*

Now, sentencing a man can vary depending on the circumstances and the judge. There's a couple of judges here that add their own conditions to the probation program just about every time. Then again, there's some that don't, other than ordering him to pay restitution or a fine or court costs or something like that. But the ones that do, they usually, well, they're not specific; like I said, they're conditions that we already have on them anyway, and they're not doing anything but putting the same ones on them.

Handling payment of restitution is one of the biggest gripes here. They don't work that out; they just say you're to pay restitution to Joe Blow in the amount of so and so, and that's it. Then you have to work it out with him, making sure he gets the money to him, and that takes a lot of time. I'd like to see them work it out some way, if they do have to pay restitution, maybe even make them pay it before they give probation. If they are going to place him on probation, boy it'd take care of that before he's sentenced.

We've also had a lot where the judge says, "I'm going to grant him probation, but I think it would be a good idea if he served a

---

*Moses William Hampton later pleaded guilty to an additional charge of possession of marijuana. His probation was revoked and he was sentenced to the state prison.

little time in jail, so I'm going to delay sentencing for a month; but I'm also going to have him remanded to the county jail until sentencing." Or, if he's got two cases, he'll sentence him—maybe he's got two grand larceny cases—he's going to put him on probation; he'll reduce one to a misdemeanor and sentence him to the county jail maybe two, three months and then after the two or three months bring him back, put him on probation on the other case. They don't do it too much because there's a conflict between the parole board and the judges. In effect, if they did that, say, "I'm going to sentence you to a year in jail and then after that I'm going to put you on probation," well they're taking the parole board's authority, because in fact they are paroling him after a year. So they do it only in a few instances where they can get around it without really being in conflict with the parole board. It's never more than two, maybe three months. That's county-jail time. They definitely couldn't sentence him out to the penitentiary and the judge say, "Well, I'm going to put you on probation after you get out."

They have a county jail, there's no hard labor to it, they keep them locked up all the time. They don't have a county farm in Mobile. Under the Alabama law you can be sentenced to the county jail up to two years. But here they never sentence anybody to more than a year over there. The facilities here, they're overcrowded. They haven't got any room for them, that's the main reason.

If they're sentenced to the penitentiary, it usually takes probably three months before they hear anything about when they will be eligible for parole. Because we have to notify the board and send them a report about their crime and background and so forth, just like a presentencing; it all takes about three months. Up until 1973 they—now everybody gets a parole hearing within a third of their time. Everybody. It used to be they didn't. That was the biggest problem. Parole. Getting a parole was easy; the biggest problem used to be for the parole board to give you a review hearing. And if they didn't let you know anything about a review hearing, you just didn't get one, and you didn't know why unless you wrote them or got some of your friends or rela-

tives or somebody to try and find out for you. But now everybody
gets one within a third of his time.

There are so many factors going on, determining his parole.
Our report we send them on his background has something to
do with it. In between the time he's in prison before he comes up
for a parole board hearing, if he's smart at all he's going to have
a lot of people writing letters to the board and going to see them,
trying to get him on parole; that has a lot to do with it, too. The
main thing though, is his conduct while he's in prison; if he's
got a lot of disciplinaries that will keep him from being paroled.
If he's finished a trade while he's been in, of course that will be
in his favor. And then, maybe the crime itself; I know even the
judge will write sometimes, even when he sentences one, and
recommends to the board that he definitely be paroled within a
third of his time.

There's so many things that work on it. That always amazes
me, because we don't ever know why the reasons were that he was
paroled. Same token, we have people come in our office all the
time and want to know how come their son wasn't paroled. He
came up within a third of his time. And there is nothing you can
tell them—you don't know. They don't let us know why they
didn't parole them, and they send the prisoner just a little notice,
"Your parole has been denied because of your prior record,"
your (what is it?) "incompatibility with society's welfare." That
covers so much, so you don't ever know why they don't parole one.

I don't know how you "get a man's attention" as a probation
officer. Most of the time I don't worry about that too much, as
far as getting on one, because unless it's a case where—well old
Moses' a case—someone needs to get his attention—and I do,
which is a problem because he just sits there. But on most of them
I don't. The only thing I feel like I can do is show them the alternatives: if you do this, there's a good chance you'll go to prison;
or if you do this you're going to lose your job. If you do this, eventually it's going to catch up with you and you won't get anywhere.
I deal mostly with just alternatives.

As far as getting someone's attention, I don't know. My father
and grandfather are in a little different situation because they

were hired and they had to work with them and there were no
two ways about it. Father had to do his job to make sure the convict did his job, and it's pretty cut and dried. Well, in a case like
that I can see where being aggressive is—it's going to have to be
the main goal. But in this situation the main thing I'm concerned
with is just making sure they're clearly aware of each alternative.
Like I was trying to let Moses know, the main thing I want to get
each one of them not to think that someone's going to lock them
in jail, which is hard to get around; it's a bad way to start any relationship. There's nothing you can do about that, you just have
to work with it. But, get them to think that when they do have a
problem there's somebody to come to.

I look at this job as law enforcement, but it's probably about
ninety/ten, eighty/twenty social work more or less. I can get on
to him all I want to and say "bullshit," which would be the truth.
That's part of his problem right here, trying to make him understand that the reason he constantly keeps getting arrested, constantly keeps getting in trouble with the law, is because he's just
too easily led by other people. Which—not all the time. Peer
group hasn't got to be bad at that age. Like I told him, there's no
way I would know each time who he's associating with and so
forth, but just make him realize that if he does associate with one
person or a type of person, then he's eventually going to get into
trouble.

Yes, I worked at Eight Mile. As a guard. The main reason I
didn't go into prison work was pretty well known all along; I just
haven't got—I won't say aggressive, that's the wrong word—but
to me, to really get on somebody like they do, which I've seen
them work; and I've also seen other guards at other prisons try
maybe a softer line, maybe like we use here, and it just doesn't
work: you're constantly getting run over. Either way. Well, that's
being a little unfair, but it just doesn't work. You've still got to
have both of them; you got to have more or less a strong arm, and
then if you want to rehabilitate anybody you're going to have to
work from an authoritative position. When I saw right off that
I'm just not that way, as far as using authority, working from
authority—I just can't really work anything that way—so, that's

the main reason I didn't want to go into corrections. There were other reasons, too. I've seen my father and grandfather, too, and that's a job that weighs on you pretty hard all the time. This one does, too, but it's in a different situation. Like, when I leave the office here, I still get calls and all at night, but I can pretty well pick up and forget it for a while. But I notice they don't; it's constantly on their minds because a twenty-four hour job is; if anything happens in there it's their responsibility. But, getting back to it, the main reason is just because I saw right off I wasn't going to be able to use authority like they do. I mean it's just not in me, as far as I can see, and I just don't feel comfortable with it. And a probation officer's job is a lot different. Like I said, most of it is primarily social work. Of course, there's a lot of people still in our department who'll go out and argue it's not, but for the most part it's in that direction.

There wasn't too much in college because I had criminology. In college it's all theory, and actually I don't really believe sociology or criminology is all that good a background for this job, because it's difficult to apply it with a large case load. I think more of rehabilitative counseling, along that line, it's a lot better if the case load isn't too large. The federal courts have set a guideline stating a maximum case load shouldn't exceed fifty per supervisor. Every book I've ever read in college also said fifty was the maximum. But that goes back to theory again. In practice, you don't have enough money, people, or the time. Criminology gives you a good background, like a lot of the criminology courses I had at South Alabama were geared both in sociology and psychology and in law enforcement; you need a lot of law-enforcement background in this job, more or less just to keep up with what they're doing; you come in contact with it, what's going on in court, like what is *nolle prosequi*. Factual stuff—you're just going to have to learn it. We got two probation officers now that have no background at all in law enforcement; they do have a little in social work. I would say they're having more problems than somebody who came in the other way—no social work but law enforcement—because you're using the terms and terminology and you're always in contact with it. And social work, to me, is a little easier to pick up. It's a lot more flexible. But really I didn't get this even, more or less, until I got with this department—we go to training sessions—and that's the attitude I'm still in.

Actually, the work at Eight Mile really wasn't as a guard. I worked there while I went to school. Summers. I went to four quarters a year and never would take a summer break, but I'd work there at night. I was more or less a replacement. As far as thinking of a guard, carrying a gun and so forth, it wasn't quite that way at the camp; I'm sure Daddy explained that. It was more or less supervision. I did that about three months. I graduated from college in June of '72. I was lucky, I graduated on a Sunday, but Tuesday before I graduated I went for an interview for this job and they told me they would let me know, and I got a letter Monday after I graduated and they offered me to report to work the next Monday, so that's the only job I even looked for. Two years after I started I had friends still out scrounging around trying to find a job.

Actually, I just went to college. I didn't know what I was going to major in. I probably should have had a football scholarship, I guess. I got offered a couple, but they were small colleges and all my friends, a bunch of us, we all decided we were going to Hattiesburg, Mississippi Southern. My intentions were to go out for football when I went over there, but you're away from home for the first time and you get to drinking beer—you could buy it anywhere—so I never did. And my grades fell off, so I transferred back to Mobile, to South Alabama. I didn't know what I was going to do. I was going to major in history at one time; well, I did get a major in political science, too, and I took all those courses in my freshman and sophomore years because they were just interesting and I hadn't decided on a major or anything. What really made me decide on this work was I got a grant: I could get a grant so long as I worked at the camp as a guard, and if I went into law enforcement it wouldn't cost me anything on my tuition; it would be free. LEAA. As long as I remained in law enforcement work for four years following graduation. I just went into that more or less because there was a good possibility;

then I started deciding I probably would go into this kind of work anyway. The LEAA is Law Enforcement Assistance Agency—a federal fund. It's a law-enforcement funding program that started back in the Johnson administration. Oh, heck they have so much money, it's unbelievable. All police departments get a share of it, and our department gets a large share. Matter of fact, three of our new people are paid on federal funds, which are LEAA.

My degree is in criminal justice and political science. Double major. So, this was pretty new to me. If you had a good background in psychology or sociology, it wouldn't be too big. Mainly psychology. I had a few psychology courses, but not really enough for a minor. Now I'm studying for a master's in correctional counseling. That's what they call it. It's just rehabilitative counseling, and since it's a new program, they're trying to direct it just toward people in probation and parole, youth services, juveniles, and the Board of Corrections.

There's twenty-four of us in the program and they all work for the parole board; none of the other organizations took up on it the first time around. It's three days a month for two years. At Troy State University; the extension is in Montgomery, and they just opened a whole new department for this under a Law Enforcement Assistance Agency grant. I kind of look, actually, in maybe the next three or four years it will be a requirement of this department that you have a master's. They're going to have to raise the salaries some more, there's no doubt about that. But, that's coming. I would say now, out of these people they hired recently, out of thirty-five—that's just approximate—I would say fifteen of them have a master's or are about to complete a master's program.

But, going back to my daddy's type of work. I've seen a lot of convicts under my father who thought the world of him. If they felt like they would do anything to hurt him, they'd just rather die, which does have its merits, it definitely does. But it could be too big a dependency sometimes. Too bad you never were around when he really got into one, though! Shoooo! I don't ever remember Papa Dees getting on but one, and that was one of the flunkies that worked around his house. He did something wrong. He climbed all over him. But I've heard my father many a times get on them. And, I thought, oh, I'd hate to be in his shoes. It was verbal with the eye contact and threats, constantly moving around. He could sure lay one on him, though.

Oh, he used to get on to me sometimes like that, too, but he could do it with a convict and not be mad. But, usually when he got on to me he was—well, he might not have been—but he gave me the impression he meant business. But I've seen him get on a convict, and if he didn't know my father, he'd think he was fixing to kill him. That convict's dead. And then when the convict would leave, he'd be laughing. But sometimes it would get to him and he really would get mad. Like I said, it does work, though.

When I was between six and eight we lived at Grove Hill. We lived a pretty good piece from the camp, I guess about six or seven miles, but we used to go over there all the time with my father. In fact, every Saturday and Sunday we went to camp and the interesting thing, we had a flunkie; I don't remember his name now—Spur, or something like that. We were going to fly. We built a kite—he happened to build a kite, the convict did— but we didn't have no spool. So the convict said, "I'm going to go ask your father if he'll let me in the warehouse and get some string and we'll string the kite up." So, he went in and my father said, "Hell no, stay out of that warehouse." So I went and asked him and he said no, you can't have no string. So we just went and got some anyway, about thirty minutes later. And my father had left and came back and we had the kite way up in the air. You know, my father got out of the truck and went over there and kicked that convict's ass, more or less just turned him over his knee and beat him, and I was—shooo, he ain't going to whup me—and then he took me inside and wore my ass out! Equal treatment for the same crime; we shared it! I was about seven, I guess. Something like that.

At Grove Hill I used to go there during the day and they always used to have some flunkies that stayed around the camp. One of them, interesting, he didn't know how to read, and I was in the first and second grade and of course had these little readers and

PRISONERS BEING MARCHED TO WORK IN THE FIELDS AT THE G. K. FOUNTAIN COR-
RECTIONAL CENTER, FORMERLY ATMORE PRISON FARM.

he asked me one time to bring those up there and help him read
them. So we'd sit out there and he would read it, and I couldn't
read too much and we'd try to make them out, and then we would
play baseball the rest of the day. They'd be hanging up laundry
and while they hung up laundry they would stop and hit me a
fly ball. Shoot, I used to enjoy going up there all the time. If you
grow up there you're never scared; I never was scared to go back
there any time.*

We moved to Mobile in '64, so I must have been thirteen or
fourteen. Daddy had worked down here at Eight Mile a long time
and I used to come down all the time; it was right down the road.
We used to spend a lot of time down there. When I was playing

---

*Fred, Sr.: "I never had any concern about Little Fred's safety. None
whatsoever. Now, I did whup them both over that kite flying because
the convict thought he could get by because Little Fred wanted to go do
it, but I just whupped both of them and got it over with. I didn't whup
the convict; I talked to him, let's put it that way!"

football in high school, during the summer I would work out
with weights, and I'd keep the weights down at the camp and
work out with them. Play basketball. The inmates used weights,
too. And I'd just leave them down there and more or less when
I went to work out, I'd have somebody to work out with. And they
would use them all the time. And I got a basketball goal and instead of putting it up at the house I took it down there and put
it up. You know, the convict camp, when you're that age, you
don't have to scrounge around to find someone to play basketball.
Just go down to the camp. And we used to play football all the
time, too. Touch.

When I got to be a guard, though, then I used to take them
out and play basketball and football and so forth, and I learned
right off, if it's a small number, maybe four or five of you went
out, that's okay—when the group's small; but when you take a
bunch of them out you can't play because they're constantly
arguing and bickering and so forth. And you're on a side? You
can't take a side on them, so I had to quit then and just referee.

It's true, one way to relieve the prison overpopulation would
be to parole more convicts, but they're paroling more now than
they ever have. They just can't keep up with it. They've bent the
rules and regulations on your paroles. They've got to where they
parole them early now. And the parole board is catching a lot of
criticism now for that reason. And the reason they've been doing
it, so they say, is to help the Board of Corrections relieve their
overcrowded situation.

It's difficult to say what the recidivism rate is. We tried to figure it up just in my office, and I guess a parolee going back is
about—maybe 20 percent of them go back. Probationers, it would
probably be 25 percent of them that don't make it. Most of the
probationers here, when they go through Circuit Court, they've
been given a prison sentence and it's been suspended. The Board
of Corrections is trying to do something now about their problem,
but I don't look for them to get any money, either.*

---

*Nearly two years after this comment, on January 13, 1976, Alabama
voters approved a $15-million bond issue of which $6 million would go
into a prison-building fund.

The case load I've got is 95 percent black, and I've got one hundred and twenty-five now. All right, the territory next to me, the probation officer there has 95 percent white. Out of my case load of one hundred and twenty-five I've got about fifty parolees and the rest probationers. He's got about twenty-two or twenty-three parolees and the rest of them are probationers.

So you can see how the blacks go to the penitentiary a lot more than whites do. It would make you think maybe there's a double standard of justice somewhere along the line, but it's really about even as far as—if a white violates his probation, he's got a better access to a lawyer—there's a good chance he can beat the case before it comes up, before it gets to the grand jury—and a black doesn't. He's got a court-appointed attorney and they don't—unless they can milk a little money out of him, too—they're not going to defend him too much. So that has a lot to do with that, too, when you say who violates probation more, black or white. I guess really, without that factor it would be about the same.

If drugs weren't a problem, weren't against the law, shoot, that other probation officer wouldn't have nothing, he wouldn't have a case load but about twenty-five. Most of the white areas are drug charges. That's the reason I didn't want it. When we got all these new supervisors and were switching territories around? I could have got a predominately white area, but I didn't want it. They're hard drugs. I've got a few drug cases, maybe ten or twelve, and that's all I want because they're a lot different to work with, because you keep thinking the only reason they're a criminal, the only law they've even thought about violating, the only flaw really they have, is drugs; and when you—if you got a burglar, he generally knows he's done something wrong and you can work from there—but somebody on drugs, 'specially marijuana, they don't see anything wrong with it. They don't feel like they have a problem or anything.

I've got to where I know a little bit about every one of my one hundred and twenty-five. I work with them, and there's some of them that don't need any supervision, really. They're going to do pretty good anyway, so some of them you don't worry about too much. You just make more or less sure they send their reports in, and maybe go by and talk to them every now and then. And

then, on the other hand, I've got some I feel like—like I've got
one drug addict, he's been through every—we've got three sorts
of drug rehabilitation homes. He's been through all three of
them and no drug involved; that wasn't the reason he was kicked
out. It was just his attitude, and they kicked him out of all three
of them. Mental health, vocational rehab, they couldn't do anything with him. He just wouldn't cooperate with them, so the
only thing I'm doing with him, I just go by and see him about once
a week, make sure he stays around town, give him a urinalysis
every now and then to see if he's off drugs. There's not much
else I can do with him 'cause there's no more programs left. And
he's been in prison several times.

     The two women probation officers here have a case load just
like everybody else. The county, we split the county up in nine
different areas, geographically and according to the size of the
case load in one area, and they just took a hunk just like everybody
else did. Like the little one, Mary, she has the territory I used to
have. There's a lot of blacks there. However, it's in a state of flux
and there's a high rate of crime there. I would think, well, it's
not the worst case load, but it's one of the bad ones and it's predominately black, and I don't think she has more than four or
five females.
     I do think it's a bigger burden on them than it would be on a
male probation officer—actually, on both the officer and the
probationer. On her and any probationer or parolee she has
because it's just—here it seems like it's just natural since they've
been here. Say I had a parolee six or eight months and I had a
pretty good relationship with him and we got to where we could
talk a little bit, well, naturally, if I just gave him to somebody else
he wouldn't like that anyway, but in a situation where you turned
him—a male parolee that you know pretty well—and you turn
him over to a female that he doesn't know anything about and
she's a female, too, he doesn't like that at all. For some reason the
probationer is more scared of female officers than they are of
us, even to the point of their putting them in jail and so forth.
     Yes, I would think a male probation officer could counsel a
woman parolee as well as a female probation officer, but it would

be pretty hard. I had a female probationer, black, and she came in one day and I wanted her to go to Mobile Mental Health; I had already arranged an appointment for her. She didn't keep the appointment; she came down here, and the problem was she was pregnant and she just didn't want to tell me. I could see it. I didn't know right off that's what it was, so we talked awhile and eventually she said that was the thing, she was pregnant, she just didn't want to tell me about it. And, I don't know, if it had been a female I'm sure she would have told her quicker than me, I don't know. But I think you can counsel both of them about the same.

It's just like anything else, once you build a good relationship with somebody, even if it is in a position like this, it shouldn't be an obstacle. I think it would be harder to build that relationship—for her opening up, me being male—but I wouldn't think it would be too much after that. But, Mary had the same problem. One of them wasn't working and he told Mary he was sick and of course she wanted to know what was wrong with him and he had a hernia and he just wouldn't tell her, and finally Mary said, "Will you tell Mr. Dees—you know him—will you tell him what's wrong?" And he said, "Yeah, I'll tell him." And so he came in here and told me what was wrong. He was just bashful to talk. But you don't run into that too often.

As far as methods of counseling, we're kind of divided here. A couple here have master's in counseling, but anyway we're always arguing about which approach to take in counseling. I take the less direct approach rather than all the time giving him instructions, telling him what to do. More or less just trying to talk with him, lead him and show him if he does that, what's going to happen. I realize that giving a man probation or parole instructions by necessity is direct.

All right, a few here are very direct. Which, to me is not too much different from just discipline. Because you tell him this is the way it is. You do it, and that's it, rather than working so much on feeling, just finding out more or less the facts, and telling them this is the way it's going to be. It works, but it's mainly on discipline.

There was a probation officer, he was big on law enforcement, and when he had one come in he kept a brick in one side of his drawer and a gun in the other one. When he wanted to reiterate a point he would take the brick out and slam it on the desk or take his gun out and say that's the way it's going to be, and things like that. They got rid of him finally. I think he went back into the service. He was in the active Guard and went into active duty. If a war comes along, I know who will be happy! He was something else. I had all his cases that he had had before, and some of them liked him, some of them loved him because he went out of his way to help them, but some of them hated him. Boy, they couldn't stand him. And when I got there, it was just a carryover. They figured I wasn't any better than him and one would go off; they would come in and say, "Mr. Dees I come in to pick up my gun," and I'd say, "What are you talking about?" He'd say, "Yeah, when I was put on probation Mr. So-and so came out to my house one night and got all my guns, he said he'd give them to me when I went off probation, so I came to get my gun." I finally got in touch with him; he'd given them to one of the sheriffs. They went by and picked up the guns. But, he'd go in the house, he'd go see them about four o'clock in the morning and go in the house, get all the guns, check around and see if they had any liquor stuff. Under Alabama law we have the authority to do that! 'Course, four o'clock in the morning, I'd be scared I'd get shot if I went into somebody's house.

This is just my observation, but I would think the main problem in the prison system is they try to carry on rehabilitation on one hand and at the same time they operate guards and security and so forth on the basis of back when my grandfather was there. People are more smart now; prisoners they get probably still don't have the average education but they're still intelligent, and it's hard for them to have a counselor on the one hand, spending two hours in a group counseling session and he's really showing them he cares and they're really talking over how they feel about things; and then it's just like throwing cold water on them when they put them back in the prison population and you go back to the old thing, strictly security and everybody's treated alike—it doesn't matter, any individual differences, everybody's the same.

I think that's the main failure they have. I don't see how you can put those two things together quite like that. You can argue that you have to have security, but on the basis like that, I would feel like anything you do in rehabilitation, most of it would be lost when you put them back in the security thing. And another thing, another concept that a lot of people have and the parole board does, too, if you've had a lot of disciplinaries in prison that doesn't necessarily mean you are going to have a hard time making it on parole because some people just can't adjust to that up there.

I'd like to see it, maybe—well some people who go to prison I don't think should be released. They should have to sit there the rest of their lives, but they should put it in a way where they have one big prison, maybe Holman, that's maximum security, and that would be the lifers, the psychopaths, maybe third offenders. Put them together, that's it; there's no need putting them in with everybody else.

The first offenders, maybe even the second offender, they haven't reached the point of no return. For them maybe build, oh heck, several prisons with a population of no more than two hundred and kind of spread them out, throughout the state, and have your rehabilitation going on there. And another thing they'd have to have, which is beginning to start here, is some contact with the community. It's a little late; they've started it, but it's a big change going from prison back outside, and they need some way where they can have contact with the community, maybe work release; if nothing else, maybe even a parole officer go talk to them or something, some contact, something to expect. You've got to have something to show them somebody is going to be on their side when they get out—somebody will be working for them. Within the Department of Corrections.

Even the Link Society is okay. That's something. My gripe about them is they go off on a tangent about radical guards killing people out at Atmore and they forget about things as far as arranging home plans, following up on their families while they're in prison, or helping them find a job, making sure they have

field workers who do go by and counsel with them, show them
that they leave all that behind. But, they're off this way hollering
about they're not spending enough money, or they're giving
too much money to the guards, or the guards have a death list.
And that's all that gets to the public, it's just that part of it. To my
way of thinking they shouldn't spend so much time on that, and
that's the reason they have such a bad name; nobody here likes
them. The reason I don't like them and the reason they don't
either, and it's a legitimate gripe, they put us in difficult situations
a lot of times by grouping us with law enforcement. They've even
told some of our parolees, "If you have a problem come and see
me, don't worry about seeing your parole officer; he's going to
try and put you in prison." And they'll work job situations out;
we'll get somebody who's coming out on parole and the Board
of Corrections will send us a letter saying so and so is going to
live with his mother and he's going to work for so and so; this
job has been provided by the Link Society.

Most of the convicts that I've talked to are real cynical about
the rehabilitation program. I honestly believe there are people
that work in the prison that can't have help; most of them have
picked up a trade or went through trade school, but they're still
cynical about it because they know themselves that the only way
you're going to get anything in prison is to put the hat on folks.
You have to cheat and lie and so forth even to just stay alive, more
or less, and they're real cynical. I haven't had a one come out
and say, "I really learned a lot in prison, it's helped me a lot, it's
straightened me out all together." I think most of them, if the
prison does anything for them, it's in spite of more than because of.
The funny thing about it, I honestly believe, I don't care how
many times they've been out, at least for the first week, maybe a
month, they are going straight. You could sit here all day and
try to talk one of them into committing burglary or take a drug
or something and he wouldn't do it. But then it wears off. And
that's the main problem I think we have, we don't realize maybe
within the first six months how much time we should spend with
them. And the discipline wears off a whole lot faster—a lot faster.
It takes more to get accustomed to nobody telling them when

they got to eat and when they go to sleep and so forth, but they get back in the swing of things pretty quick.

I put myself in the same position, and I've been in prison, let's say three years, haven't had a woman, haven't had a real good time, and I get out and I say, "I can't do that because if I do I might get in trouble and I might go back to prison," but eventually that's going to wear off. They're going to come back into contact with the people they used to associate with. It might not have been a bad association with people they knew on the street and so forth, and they're going to get back into that thing. The main thing, the main problem, is the ones we have less success with, is the ones who don't have anybody when they get out. Maybe their wife's left them, or their families live somewhere else and they just got a good job here and that's the reason they can't—those types don't have anything to hang onto—they don't usually make it, which is understandable. If you felt like you didn't have anybody who cared anything for you, everything was going pretty bad, naturally you'd get to where you wouldn't give a shit.

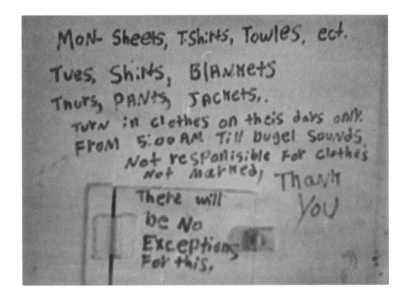

INDEX

ALABAMA PRISONS TODAY
*A portfolio of photographs
by Brad Fisher*

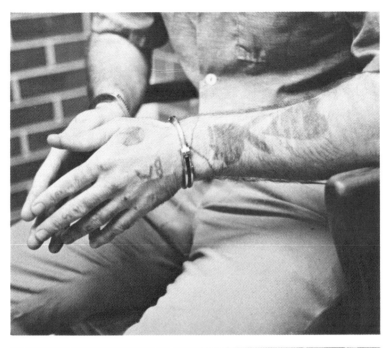

ALABAMA BOUND
was composed in VIP Baskerville by
Chapman's Phototypesetting, Fullerton, California,
printed by McNaughton-Gunn, Inc., Ann Arbor, Michigan,
and bound by Kingsport Press, Kingsport, Tennessee.
Editors: Morgan L. Walters and Francis P. Squibb
Production: Paul R. Kennedy
Book design: Anna F. Jacobs